AMERICA
ON THE
PRECIPICE

*Practical Truths for
Saving America Today*

JEFFREY P GORMAN

outskirtspress

DENVER, COLORADO

Outskirts Press, Inc.
http://www.outskirtspress.com

ISBN: 978-1-4787-1916-8

Outskirts Press and the "OP" logo are trademarks belonging to Outskirts Press, Inc.

PRINTED IN THE UNITED STATES OF AMERICA

This book is dedicated to my family:

My wife Tammy, Kids- Megan, Katie, Hunter, Arianna and Toby. Mom and Dad, brother and sisters.

Thanks you for your patience in putting up with me all these years.

Contents

Introduction

REMEMBER THE BUMPER stickers that appeared right after the 2008 November elections that said," Is it 2012 yet?"? Well now it's here or already passed, depending on when you picked up this book. Time to make some decisions and action based on what we've learned.

So.... How do we save America...or is there nothing wrong with it? There are many ways of looking at that question and a blanket statement is not really going to do the issue justice. This is much like looking at a political candidate or party and saying that their philosophy is the "right" one. There will never be a candidate or party that does everything right or everything in a way that any one person will agree on. So, I am going to put forth what I think needs to be done to fix this mess.

I have done my best to compile the most factual and common sense plan to make things work as best as possible, to get back to our country's roots and also to be fair to all. That is not to say I have covered everything or taken everything into account. I welcome any alternate opinions or additional support for what I have presented. You can contact me at http://jeffreypgorman.wordpress.com/ or e-mail to **jeffreypgorman@gmail.com.** We can carry on discussions and meet again online or in the pages of another book.

Is the country really a mess? Is there something fundamentally wrong with America? At its core... No... this is the greatest county in the world and has a solid framework set down by the founding fathers that is so flexible and well put together with its checks and balances and the ability to modify our constitution that this nation should be able to weather any storm and do just fine indefinitely.

So why are we having so many problems? Essentially, the core values of this country have been forgotten, and we as citizens have allowed this to happen. As a nation, Americans have been so fortunate and in many ways so financially blessed that we can afford to distract ourselves and enjoy our lives not concerning ourselves with politics or government in which our elected officials are so capable of handling for us...right? WRONG!

Does it look like our elected officials have done a good job running the ship? The government has gone so far off track that we are in a crisis that is threatening to take down the great nation which, maybe, some of us can still remember. Our founding fathers set a foundation to ensure it would not happen but yet we have allowed it to occur anyway by purposely ignoring the core values and documents that built it in the first place.

Corruption, self-serving agendas and of course, MONEY , have slowly but surely led our elected officials and their hired personnel away from their required duties and into other endeavors, interests and whatever else you might call it. For instance Politicians wrote the laws exempting them from telling the truth in political advertising so if we rely on these ads to make our decisions without intensive research on our own, we cannot possibly make a good decision. An MIT poll in August 2012 shows that the Presidential campaign ads running this summer are less than 42% accurate in the supposed facts they portray. So essentially they are 58% lies and we are supposed to rely on this to pick our leader. Good voting requires a lot of work on our part but we need to push for the requirement that ads be true and factual.

Over time this became business as usual and a very well engrained, powerful system has arisen to keep the ball rolling down the wrong side of the hill. That hill, which President Ronald Reagan once said, we were the "great shining city" sitting on top of. All the while... the grasshopper plays......So let's get started...

CHAPTER 1

Government Spending

WHAT CAN WE say about government spending that hasn't already been shouted from the mountaintops?

We have a trillion dollar deficit. What!? You have got to be kidding?!

No, we aren't unfortunately. What is being done about this in the national government? Not a lot, apparently. For starters The Federal Government has not passed a budget in three years. How can the government spend within their limits if they don't even set a limit? The debt ceiling is a good limit but they keep changing it. How can it be a limit if you can just change it? Many states have a balanced budget requirement. The federal Government should pass a balanced budget amendment with an exception in times of declared war or emergency defense.

I watch on TV the arguing and bickering and finger pointing and well, Idiocy, quite frankly. Isn't this really a bunch of elementary school mathematics when you get right down to it?

1+1 = 2 . 1+1 does not equal 3 ½, except on Capitol Hill.

They debate, they make cases for each side, some credible, some ridiculous. How many of the American citizens can tell the difference? The end results show that many in Congress may not, or are they lying to us for their own end? Do they care? Much of the legislation is politically motivated grandstanding, buying time until the next election or pleasing just enough people, just long enough, to win that election. Then who cares what happens? It is the next President's problem, the next Congress, the next generation. They get their pension either way. One Congressman even stated in Readers Digest that the decision making is really done off of the house floor. The speakers on the floor are all for show, especially with TV, so we don't even get to see the real government at work if we take the time to watch.

This book takes a look at different pieces of this problem individually so the government spending section will be a little more high level.

If I were elected President, I would say in my first speech:

"As your elected President of the United States, in order to gain control of our deficit and government spending, effective immediately, all government departments and offices will reduce their budget by 5%. Your next disbursement of funds from the federal government will be 5% smaller than the last so you will need to make adjustments immediately. No current positions of employment may be cut to achieve this goal."

It's not earth shattering but it is a starting point. In a 14 trillion dollar budget, that is an overnight reduction of $700 Billion. That is close to the same figure that was issued in President Obama's first big stimulus and maybe, erases that expenditure. Of course, in accounting speak, that stimulus is a "sunk cost", it's gone and now we clean up the mess. Some essential government functions may be affected by this and some may get a pass on this initial cut but optional services will soon be informed that their cut will be increased to 10% to compensate for the lack of cuts elsewhere.

I say not to cut any jobs yet because with unemployment at or near double digits the last thing we need is to move the cost of productive positions into the unemployment compensation bucket. The government is still paying money either way. Let these people begin to think about their futures and move on at their own pace to private jobs or to areas of the government that might be more essential, at least for now. Jobs, offices, services and maybe departments will eventually need to go.

Here's is another idea, next time due to budget problems, the government threatens to shut down for a few days or allow all non-essential employees take some time off, make a note of who stays home. Maybe when job cuts are the next step in the process, these positions should go away. Why is the "limited" federal government, as set up by the founding fathers, employing non-essential personnel anyway?

What do we cut in relation to services and departments? The government has grown so large and so many people are used to so much from the government that some of it will never go away. We need a strategy to get people used to the idea that many of these things will disappear and so they need to figure out how to deal with it.

First we need to find out where duplication of services is being done and consolidate departments or services. For instance the Department of Homeland Security is a complete duplication of what the FBI, CIA and National Transportation Safety Board are already doing. Expand those groups if you must but don't add another department. There must be rampant duplication throughout the welfare health and human services and other departments. Let's make a list of these.

Second, reduce federal waste. This is something the government needs to commit themselves to and every federal employee does their part to make sure it happens. This is something that needs to take place in normal daily operation and can hardly be done from outside. Start reducing the budgets of each group and they will find a way. Employees that don't make reducing waste and fraud a priority need to be let go.

Also federal employees should not make more than their private counterparts. Government service should be for people who want to serve their country not look for a cushy place to be secure and make more than the private workers who need to work their tail off for every penny.

We want to get back to the core of the Constitution but there are some good things that are not in the scope of the Constitution that also make our country pretty special. In 2012, can we imagine a life without our grandparents getting Social Security and Medicare? Isn't it great to have Unemployment Compensation in the event the rug gets pulled out from under you? Welfare may be the equivalent of long term care insurance for those who are not actually disabled. However, all of these have been abused, maligned and broken. We will talk more about these later. In their slimmest, trimmest forms they can probably stick around.

Many government programs for philanthropy may need to be scaled back or eliminated. Arts programs and the like are great to have but should probably be funded by those who use them. The fear is the general public may not be willing to pay for these things out of their own pocket. Then why is the federal government using money taken from their pockets to fund these things? They must not be that important to most people. People will fund what they feel is important or lose it. If it is not that important to the public, then it should not be helping to push our country toward total bankruptcy.

Take what he government does and compare it to what a business does. Take governmental operations and compare them to what you do as a family. If you ran your business or your household the way the federal government runs would it last long? Months? A few years maybe...

The Federal Government has been on the same track for almost a century now. How much time do you think we have left? Months? A few years .... Maybe...

Earlier this year on January 13, 2012, nine nations in the Eurozone, including France, Italy, Spain and Portugal, received severe credit downgrades. These countries have enormous debt and are being asked to bail out other nations such as Greece which are failing.

Crippled countries can't bail out a defaulting one. The United States also received a credit downgrade. This is a global crisis that needs to be taken seriously. Very few nations have strong economies except the growing third world. If we do not want to see a dramatic shift of power and prosperity away from the west, we need to wake up.

The world economy has always been able to count on US consumer spending to pick up and boost businesses in Europe and Asia which produce goods and services that we consume in the United States. Unfortunately, with the net worth of the average American dropping an average of 39% over just a few years, US consumer spending has not rebounded significantly. The world has not gotten the usual boost from the US and their economic model is collapsing.

Most of Europe typically has slow growth and very expensive governmental support of the population. That is a model that needs to be reworked by reducing vacation time and unemployment compensation periods while increasing the retirement age.

Some countries in Europe average more than five weeks' vacation time per year, unemployment periods measured in years rather than weeks, retirement ages in the Fifties and free health care, when you can eventually get in to be seen. Worldwide this model has reached its breaking point and needs to be scrapped.

At the same time Europe is being forced to move away from these things, the United States federal government is trying to move toward that model with the help of labor unions. Some states have government workers who can retire with a pension after 20 years. If these workers started right out of high school they'd be ready to retire at age 38! With the rising life expectancy, the old model of 30 year pensions should be revised where pensions still exist. Most people work over 40 years now so that should be the new standard for full pension however with the frequency of job changes, graduated pensions based on time served, starting at 20 years, similar to the military would be a better plan. Workers would still need to put in 40 years to get a full pension but it would be divided amongst 2 or 3 employers or one small pension and a 401K from another.

All workers should be required to pay into their pension funds and healthcare. There has been such whining from employees including those in Wisconsin with recent changes to laws there. People think paying even 5% of their benefits is unreasonable. There are many in this country, especially the self-employed who pay for 100% of their own benefits and a majority of this country now pay 80-100% of the money going into their retirement accounts with no assurance that it will all be there when they retire.

This expensive government model is very popular with the people of Europe and change has met with huge resistance, which we can also expect here in the US. However we must be resolute and push forward to restore America to its past years of productivity and pride.

How has Europe begun to fix their situation?

In Ireland, public service positions received an across the board 30% pay reduction, public services were cut and taxes were increased to balance out the budget. Great Britain is doing much the same to the sounds of great wailing and gnashing of teeth.

Conversely, The Greek people are more strongly resisting and the French voted out their US friendly President, Nicholas Sarkozy to keep the government gravy train running.

The Greek economy has failed and been bailed out twice. Germany like other stronger nations is resisting more bailouts and possibly reverting back to the Deutschmark. Once Italy and Spain begin having runs on the banks for fear of losing their money, the Euro economy is in grave trouble.

In 2012 and forward, what will the United States of America do?

Deficit reduction plans proposed recently have set 10 year timelines to eliminate the deficit, which is crazy. Did they do the calculations on this? As of September 2012 we have a 16 trillion dollar debt, adding one trillion each year, 3.88 billion per day. I don't know what interest rate we pay on this debt but we'll guess 3%. If they cut spending by 100 billion dollars each year to eliminate the deficit in ten years, the debt will have increased to around 24 trillion dollars before the budget is balanced. The US Gross Domestic Product is just over 15 trillion dollars. There is no possibility of recovering from this and paying off 24 trillion dollars of debt. Deep cuts need to be made immediately to balance the budget in 2 or three years. This is scary at the depth that cuts need to occur but it needs to happen. Raising taxes will most likely also be necessary because the cuts may be too painful but tax increases can't happen right now because the economy is too weak.

Coming up fast is the "Fiscal Cliff" which the federal government seems unable to prevent. This would be the expiration of the Bush tax cuts passed in 2001 costing many families several thousand dollars per year. Child tax credit would decrease $400 per child, taxes on dividends rise from 15% to 35% and capital gains from 15% to 20%. The expiration of the Obama payroll tax holiday would raise payroll taxes back to 2009 levels increasing taxes by 2% per worker.

The result is predicted to be a 3% contraction in the economy due to loss of liquid cash to the working public. Considering the economy is only growing at 1-2 percent annually this would translate into a... you guessed it....Recession!, the dreaded double-dip.

The government is close to the debt limit and will want to raise that again. Between the two issues it is predicted that the US will suffer another bond rating drop. This will be very damaging. Countries that have had a second rating drop have taken 10-20 years to regain their rating. Canada was the fastest regaining theirs after 10 years. Kudos to them! Why don't we just take action in advance and save ourselves the stress.

Congress needs to get on the stick and lock themselves away to pass a budget that will within 3 years provide a surplus and begin to pay down the national debt. The situation is so bad; the swing from here to there will be like Wile E Coyote swinging across the canyon. We need to act fast to avoid smacking into the fiscal wall. The trip won't be very pretty but ten years from now when the United States has a Triple A bond rating and a budget surplus with no debt, we'll all be standing proud of what we've done.

A big question: do we take on more debt keeping the tax cuts in place to stimulate the economy, raising the debt ceiling and risk another bond rating downgrade? The answer is spending cuts. Keep the tax reductions and cut spending to stave off the debt ceiling increase. Keeping taxes lower will allow unemployment to stay lower and reduce unemployment compensation costs.

A great way to cut costs in the federal government is to stop wasting time and money holding Congressional hearings on every little thing that happens in this country. Why are they holding congressional hearings on things that are none of the government's business like: steroid use in baseball, song lyrics in popular music, and whether or not automobile executives fly in private planes? Cut out the garbage and just do your jobs. If someone is committing a crime have the District Attorney charge them and send them to court.

Department of Corrections:

How many times have you heard debates on whether to spend money on new prisons, they are overcrowded, criminals are bored and dangerous and the recidivism rate is too high. Here's an idea that can seriously reverse this situation.

The US Navy submarine sailors share bunks. They sleep in three shifts 8 hours apiece. Why is this good enough for the US Navy but can't be done in our prisons?

Put the prisoners to work on anything useful they can produce and pay them very little if anything for the effort. They will work 12 hour shifts, 7 days per week in rotation, with one sleeping and two at work around the clock. This will leave 1 hour break each for breakfast, lunch, dinner and a shower before bed. Then they can have the balance of the shower hour to watch TV or read. They will have no time for gangs, fighting or boredom.

The money saved on labor having prisoners do this work rather than highly paid state or federal employees will likely pay for the prison, not to mention housing three times the prison population with no crowding. We will not need to build more jails. This will also be deterrent to additional crime because criminals who don't mind going to jail now will begin to realize they are working their tails off for no pay in prison and would be better off on the outside working legitimate 8 hours a day for real pay plus the freedom to do as they wish the other 16 hours.

Additionally, In order to rehab these prisoners, first time offenders will be tested in literacy and math upon entry and passing a proficiency exam will be a condition of their release. They can be given training in basic skills in lieu of some work hours and maybe put on clerical tasks. In this way they will gain knowledge, skills and confidence to reduce the likelihood of ending back in jail. Illiteracy and opportunity are often stated as great roadblocks for getting on the straight and narrow this should no longer be the case.

Unemployment:

One thing we need to touch on briefly which is a technical point but something we should be watching. There are six types of unemployment numbers called U-1 thru U-6. Each statistic includes a larger group of Americans depending on how you want to look at the data. The typical unemployment number reported by the US Government is the U-3 figure which according to the Bureau of Labor Statistics is **Total unemployed, as a percent of the civilian labor force (official unemployment rate)**. This has been around 8 to 9 percent over the past four years. This is a high number since a time of no unemployment is considered around 3 or 4 percent since normal job transitions will account for that many people. The U-6 number is probably more important because this includes the entire labor force. The U-6 Numbers have been in the 14-15 percent range the last 4 years and are really the true unemployment picture.

U-6 is: **Total unemployed, plus all persons marginally attached to the labor force, plus total employed part time for economic reasons, as a percent of the civilian labor force plus all persons marginally attached to the labor force.** Persons marginally attached to the labor force are those who currently are neither working nor looking for work but indicate that they want and are available for a job and have looked for work sometime in the past 12 months. Homemakers are not part of the Labor Force for purposes of calculating these figures since they are not seeking employment.

In July 2012 the U-3 unemployment numbers increased to 8.3%. This represented increases in 44 of the 50 states and remained the same in 4 states. North Dakota with its robust oil drilling business has unemployment at 3%. Three states are still in double-digit unemployment as high as 12%. If the Fiscal Cliff is realized and economy contracts, it is predicted that unemployment nationwide will be over 9% in the latter part of 2013.

Official metrics of unemployment calculations were not put in place until 1940 so the 25% figures quoted for the Great Depression are a best guess based on historical information available and are not considered accurate. No one really knows based on the U-3 and U-6 calculations what the unemployment figures were during that time but 25% is accepted as the unofficial number.

"The problem with socialism is that eventually you run out of other people's money to spend." - Margaret Thatcher

CHAPTER 2

Immigration Reform

ONE OF THE hottest topics in the media has been the issue of Immigration reform. By hot I don't just mean that there is a lot of talk on the issue, the discussion has been quite heated at times. One portion gets highly offended since this affects friends and family or members of their ethnic group, the other side believes reform is just plain common sense and cannot understand why people don't understand the situation. A third group sees personal or political gain from maintaining the status quo or assumes reform is just plain mean. I am going to put this in plain quantitative terms and a logical plan for correcting the situation.

To start, let me join the group that has nothing against immigration. My maternal grandparents were born in Ireland and came over to Ellis Island before 1910. My entire family was in Europe prior to the 1860s. In fact everyone except the American Indians emigrated at some time. Historical evidence indicates that the American Indians may have come over from Russia sometime many centuries ago. So who is really a Native American? Let's take that old debate off the table and focus on 2012 and what we have going on now.

At a high level we need to break immigrants into three groups:

1. <u>Immigrants</u> - These are the folks, who applied for immigration, waited their turn and followed the legal process. Many have taken citizenship exams and are now citizens of the United

States. These are the people that most of us are descended from.

2. Refugees - These people have fled a war torn country or escaped a brutal regime with their lives and the clothes on their back. This is a topic for another time but I believe the government needs to talk to their allies to get a plan together to deal with these situations. If a large group of people need to be evacuated we need to be able to squash the regime or scoop them up and distribute them to various partner nations for assistance and help in starting a new life. The US cannot and should not shoulder this effort alone.

3. Illegal Aliens - These are the people who for reasons of increased freedom or economic opportunity choose to come to the United States without invitation or regard for proper procedure.

In this plan we will deal with group 1 and 3 since these are two sides of the same coin. Group 2 is another issue for another time.

In this politically correct world the term "illegal alien" has been replaced with "illegal immigrant" or some other less accurate term such as "migrant worker". The problem is that "Illegal Immigrant" is an oxymoron. You cannot be called an immigrant if you come to the United States illegally.

One argument we need to debunk right of the bat is the insinuation that the battle against illegal immigration is a racial issue. It is not. We are not opposed to any specific racial, religious or ethnic group coming to America, only the means by which they do so. It should be done properly and by the accepted procedure so that they are sure to be a benefit to the United States and not a detriment.

If a person came into your house without being invited and decided to use your belongings without permission you would call the police and have them charged with breaking and entering. The federal government is obligated to do the same with the illegals that are streaming across our border or overstaying their expired visas but they have decided to neglect that obligation. Instead they have proposed amnesty legislation to do the equivalent of laying out the red carpet and setting up a buffet dinner for them. Furthermore they have filed lawsuits against states such as Arizona and Alabama who try to do the job for themselves citing that federal law supersedes state law and states cannot pass laws identical to federal laws. So, then why don't the feds do their jobs?

Today we have an estimated 11-13 million illegal immigrants in the United States, of all races creeds and colors, many of whom are accepting public assistance, public housing, public education and all are using our infrastructure, roads, water lines sewers, etc. Some may not be working at all and paying little or no taxes. Now, it is hard to avoid some taxes, such as sales tax. If you shop, you pay but the federal government does not have a sales tax. Federal tax comes mostly in the form of income tax. Income taxes are often avoided by working under the table or not working at all and receiving public assistance.

According to a study conducted by the Federation for American Immigration Reform (FAIR), the cost of illegal immigration in the United States is estimated at $113 billion a year. That's an average of $1,117 for every household in America.

At the state level the cost per state in Texas and California is greater than each State's budget deficit. Do you see an opportunity here? Remove this cost and the budget balances.

The numbers in the FAIR report show:

In Texas, the cost of immigration is equal to the state's current budget deficit of 16.4 Billion. In California, the poster child for runaway deficits, the cost of illegal immigration is $21.8 billion while the budget deficit is only $13.8 billion. California would actually have a budget surplus after subtracting the illegal immigration costs. In New York, the $6.8 billion deficit is one third less than the $9.5 billion yearly cost of its illegal population.

These numbers do include the public education of American citizens born to illegal immigrants which can be seen as either a positive or a negative. Education good - illegals bad. We will address this group in a few pages.

How can we reverse this situation? Do we put up a big fence on the border? Do we round them all up and send them home? What makes sense fiscally, realistically and morally? What about all of the families, children, multigenerational people and otherwise law-abiding immigrants?

Let me explain my plan....

We don't want to be unfair or hurt anyone, uproot longstanding relationships or create a race and class war. This can mostly be avoided if we use common sense and planning. Many people will still be offended and unreasonable about the situation. We can't worry about them. No plan will please everyone so we won't try to do that. This will be hard on many, seen as mean by others but sensible and kind by most.

First, we need to grease the skids for those that legitimately want to immigrate and have skills or value to add to the melting pot of America. People with no skills do little to help progress the American economy. Many people need to wait 10 years or more to join their immediate family in America. This is not right. Spouses, children and elderly parents of legal immigrants should be able to emigrate within a year or so. If we make it easier to emigrate legally then we can shoo away the detractors who say we are mean and unreasonable. They do not have a valid argument.

This is not to say we give amnesty to those who have already illegally crossed the border and set up shop in the States. In extreme cases which we will detail, we can put these people first in line for legal immigration but they need to be serious about it as such:

1. Temporary visas can be issued to anyone as they are now, provided they have a valid reason for travel and are not on any watch list or prohibited from international travel for any reason. An example is the H1-B Visas used for workers coming in from foreign nations as well as Travel Visas, Student Visas, etc.

2. The Citizenship exam will be offered only in English. Information on how to sign up for the test will be distributed to interested parties in their native language clearly stating that they must speak English well enough to take the exam without unusual assistance.

3. The exam will cover basics of US history, proving that the candidate understands who we are as a nation and they will sign off on acceptance of our way of life as their own. They must understand the Declaration of Independence and the Constitution as well as notable current office holders.

4. The exam will cover basics of life in these United States. What are basic laws that we live by? How do we pay taxes and what types of taxes are required.

5. Any waiting periods will be shortened and information technology used to make the process as smooth and streamlined as possible. However the total number of immigrants will be limited, so as not to not cause the total population of the United States to increase significantly. An average year will only show an increase to the total population of one percent but as the birth rate slows and the baby boomers reach the average life expectancy, some years, immigration can increase and still be below the population decrease of the country as a whole. Statistics for 2011 show the birth rate slowing to an early 1940s pace, which was during World War II.

Once this has been accomplished and we can give immigrants a way of coming in more easily, we can deal with those who won't play the game by the rules.

It is important that these people have skills and desire to be educated. A study done by the Center for Immigration Studies shows that giving amnesty to unskilled illegals increases the cost to the federal government by 300%. "If illegal aliens were given amnesty and began to pay taxes and use services like households headed by legal immigrants with the same education levels, the estimated annual net fiscal deficit would increase from $2,700 per household to nearly $7,700, for a total net cost of $29 billion." Why? Because the immigrants, now being legal, are eligible for all of the benefits illegals are not. We need to be sure these people are immediately employable to avoid this. We can't add these people to welfare, Women Infant Children sustenance program (WIC), social security, Medicare and other programs and not expect it to be expensive. They should only be allowed in if they are paying full taxes.

Also according to CIS, among the largest costs are Medicaid ($2.5 billion); treatment for the uninsured ($2.2 billion); food assistance programs such as food stamps, WIC, and free school lunches ($1.9 billion); the federal prison and court systems ($1.6 billion); and federal aid to schools ($1.4 billion).

What deterrent makes the most sense? Putting up a fence is a helpful move, slowing down the flow of immigrants across the border but as we know, you build a ten foot fence; you can bring in a 12 foot ladder. That is inconvenient and troublesome for the people but not insurmountable. We can't put enough people to watch the border so something else needs to be the primary plan. In order to stop illegals from Europe and Asia, the Middle East and other locations both the Mexican and Canadian borders would need to be fenced. Then what about boats, do you fence the beaches of the Great Lakes and the east and west coasts of the United States? The biggest problem is in Southern California and along the Rio Grande so maybe we can fence that but we need a better plan. Mexicans have boats too.

The question to ask is…. Why are they coming in the first place? If we remove the carrot drawing the flow of immigrants, we'll see fewer trying to cross the borders or swim the Rio Grande. This is equally effective for immigrants from all countries including in our northern border and ports.

Essentially they are coming for one of three things: Freedom, Opportunity or the free services and support.

We cannot remove Freedom or Opportunity. Those are inalienable rights as stated in the Constitution, you remember Life, Liberty and the pursuit of Happiness? However these are limited to Citizens of the United States. Foreigners do not have Constitutional rights in the United States. If they go through the proper channels of obtaining visas and green cards then they can enjoy the same right we have as citizens for the length of their stay. Otherwise they do not have that privilege, so in some respects we can remove it, for those who break the law.

Free services and support can easily and strictly be limited to Citizens of the United States. This we can remove totally. We can cover most of this in the chapter on Welfare but there are a couple of categories that apply here.

For the process overall we need to remove these benefits in a phased approach not yank the rug out from under people. That is not the humane way to go. The phased approach will allow time for people to make decisions on their situation and adjust accordingly to what is best for them. Leaving town will hopefully be the ultimate choice.

First off we need to revise section 1 of the 14th amendment which in its original form states....

Section 1.
All persons born or naturalized in the United States, and subject to the jurisdiction thereof, are citizens of the United States and of the State wherein they reside. No State shall make or enforce any law which shall abridge the privileges or immunities of citizens of the United States; nor shall any State deprive any person of life, liberty, or property, without due process of law; nor deny to any person within its jurisdiction the equal protection of the laws.

The 14th Amendment of the US Constitution was enacted in 1868 for the intention of protecting the rights of African Slaves who were emancipated in 1865 by the 13th Amendment. To paraphrase section 1 of Amendment 14: "Anyone born in the United States will automatically be a US citizen.".. This would allow slaves to own property and act in most ways like other US citizens. Former slave owners could not gather up ex -slaves and expel them from the country or force them to suffer any other such persecution. The question is, looking at the amendment with today's eyes, is this still appropriate? Since this is not one of the 10 amendments in the Bill of Rights, we can look at this critically to decide if changing this provision is in the best interest of America today.

The provision is still a good one today in that it eliminates some bureaucratic hassle and questions from the process of becoming a citizen. A simple birth certificate will suffice. However, the original intent of the amendment is obsolete and has opened the door to abuse by illegal immigrants which is a new problem not encountered to any great detriment in past centuries. There are no slaves in the United States today who need protected by the 14th amendment except those possibly brought here in human trafficking rings. However, there are laws on the books to prevent slavery, slave labor, child labor and the crimes committed by human traffickers, so the 14th amendment is not needed to protect individuals affected by these crimes.

Adding an amendment to modify the first section of 14th amendment would read something like this: "This provision will replace the first sentence of section 1 of Amendment 14 and specifies that any child born in the United States, will not be automatically be considered a citizen of the United States unless at least one biological parent is previously a citizen of the United States and declares their intent to have their child be a natural born citizen of the United States. Once an immigrant successfully completes the citizenship process, all of their minor children will be certified as citizens and the spouse will be allowed accelerated approval status, waiving any waiting periods in the citizenship process".

This provision will add extra difficulty in authorizing new babies as citizens but a simple amendment to the birth certificate adding the citizenship status of the parents; will return the birth certificate to being the only document necessary for citizenship verification. I believe this newly created problem of not all natural born people being authorized as citizens, is easier to resolve than the overall illegal immigration problem and thus, modifying the 14th Amendment is a key cornerstone in immigration reform.

The most effective immigration reform comes in two parts. Reforming legal immigration to make this easier for those who desire it and secondly, removing the proverbial "carrot" that draws illegal immigrants to the United States in large numbers. Having a child born in the United States automatically become a citizen, simply by crossing the border before the child's birth is a great draw for those who wish to have a foothold for public services and other benefits in the United States. This situation however, causes serious difficulty and debate for the issue of what immigrants should be deported and raises the moral question of whether you can separate families or deport a child citizen because their primary caregiver is here illegally. Forcing the parents to go through the citizenship process before their children can be declared a citizen eliminates those issues. This should reduce the pace at which immigrants come across the border. In the future, an illegal immigrant will not have citizen children to "anchor" them in the United States and splitting families along these lines is not an issue.

This is only one piece of comprehensive immigration reform but is a powerful tool to make legal immigration a more attractive option. This also simplifies enforcement of existing immigration laws making it easier to prosecute and deport those who do not take advantage of streamlined legal immigration.

Pretty simple, makes sense and works for today.

Secondly, we will require proper documentation to get valid identification. This would include drivers' licenses and other photo ID. Citizens will provide their birth certificate and social security card to get the IDs.

Third, this ID and a valid social security number will be required for all public services including, welfare, WIC, social security and voting in elections. Requiring valid ID for voting will ensure that illegals cannot vote in people who will give those benefits in exchange for their votes. This is a huge issue for the future of our country and retaining control over our own government.

There has been much debate about requiring ID for voting saying it would be unfair and disenfranchise voters. Are they joking? All these people need to do is take their birth certificate and Social Security card to the Department of Motor Vehicles and pay $25 or so for an ID card. How hard is that? If they can't prove they are citizens, then they shouldn't be voting. They say it is too hard to get to the DMV? Well, then how are they planning to get to the polling place? If a person can't get their ID to vote then they must not really care very much whether they vote or not.

Why wouldn't they have an ID anyway? You need it for nearly everything, employment, bank accounts, prescriptions, video rentals, library cards, club memberships etc. Someone without and ID card must lead an exceptionally boring life. Anyone who says that the Arizona and Alabama laws requiring immigrants to show ID is unfair is being ridiculous. American Citizens need to show ID all the time, why should an immigrant get a pass on this?

Fourth, we need to deal harshly with employers who thumb their nose at the government by giving precious jobs to people who are not eligible for them. These jobs are needed by our citizens. Remember we have nearly 15 percent of Americans out of work right now when you include those who have given up looking. Many of these undocumented will be working under the table and will not pay income taxes. This is logical because without a social security number, tax ID or some other means of getting into the IRS system you cannot file a return. I place this fourth because there are a lot of hardworking people in the country illegally who would never commit crimes to support themselves and can potentially retain their job until they can file the proper paperwork for documentation.

The final result is that once these people have lost their ability to get free food, assistance, housing or a paying job, they will either need to become criminals to support themselves or simply leave.

Education:

The last thing to revoke from them is public education. For one thing the children are not at fault here and should be educated as any other. If the parents pack up and leave then there is no need to revoke the education from the children because they will have moved on. Hopefully by this point, the remaining adults will have become properly documented and this harsh move will not be necessary.

I think cutting back on the "English as a Second Language" education funding **is** necessary. It should be called "English as a **First** language". These students should be phased into an immersion program where they will be taught English gradually but required to speak English only in class after 6 months. It should only be offered to each child for one year because that should be sufficient to get a child functionally literate through coached immersion. For those who experience unusual difficulty such as those who never speak English at home, a second year is to be offered.

One issue that is typically done on a State level that is worth mentioning is state college tuition. People are free to attend any school in the world; that is not issue. However, some states, including North Carolina have proposed allowing illegal immigrants to have *in-state* tuition rates. They must be joking?!

So, essentially a student whose parents and grandparents were born in South Carolina, and living a 45 minute drive from Charlotte, North Carolina wants to attend a college in Charlotte but needs to pay out-of-state tuition. On the other hand, a student who came over from Helsinki, Finland or Botswana last week, gets to pay in-state tuition. How can anyone justify such a proposal? Those who pay the least state taxes get equal benefit to those who pay in the most. That makes no sense at all. I welcome any explanation as to how this has any intelligence.

Deportation:

So what about those that are already here? People say round them up and send them all back but that is not realistic for reasons of both time and money. They need to be divided into four groups and prioritized by urgency and respect for our nation.

1. Newly arrived immigrants and those who have committed serious crimes. Those single people who have established no ties to the community or those who are convicted of crimes such as burglary, rape, murder, gang activity, drug distribution and other crimes will be deported as soon as they can be processed or their jail terms are over.

2. Singles or married couples and people who have been here for a few years but have not assimilated into our culture. These people have not become fluent in English or taken necessary steps to become Americans. This includes those who commit more minor crimes such as shoplifting, minor drug possession, DUI without injuries or repeated deportation.

3. Singles or married people who may have brought with them children born in their native country or who have been here 5 -10 years but committed no crimes, are functional in society and speak English well.

4. Established residents 10 years or more or who have had children born in the United States. These children and sometimes grandchildren are citizens and know no other life but being an American. These people have been law abiding and caused no serious problems for their neighbors.

These prioritization groups will start with the criminals and gang members and get them incarcerated or removed from our country as quickly as possible. All known Category One members in custody will be deported before moving to prioritization group 2 and so forth. So, if we can't actually deport them all, then those who have been here for a while and caused no trouble may never get their turn. To some extent, that is just fine. This is not intentional amnesty, just a logistical reality that we will not be able to get to them all. It may be some reward for those who choose to be a quality individual in the

United States.

Folks in category 4 will be given citizenship preparation materials and held to the same high standard as new immigrants coming legally. There will be a time limit in which they will need to complete the process, possibly one or two years or risk deportation. This should not be difficult for someone who has been here for some time. This may be viewed as amnesty but weighting the harm vs. benefit of uprooting productive, established families based on principle just does not make sense. There are true criminals to gather up and send home. Two years will provide these people the opportunity to weigh the consequences and decide if this simple procedure is worth keeping their life in America. I suspect few will refuse to follow through.

Categories One Two and Three will never be immune to deportation and due to the revision of the 14th Amendment can never be a category Four. They can leave the country and file for legal citizenship.

We can make one exception, if a category 3 or 4 individual who speaks English well wants to fast track themselves to citizenship they can file the proper paperwork for citizenship and enlist in the US armed forces. We will require them to take two sessions of basic training to help ensure any dangerous elements are weeded out and after a citizenship training class will be sent off to their unit to serve. If they complete their enlistment with an honorable discharge they can immediately take the citizenship exam. After two years of service this should be no challenge.

In the end, 11-13 million illegals can be turned into several million new taxpaying citizens while the troublemakers and those who really aren't committed to the process can be fingerprinted, recorded and sent home to try again legally. If they are found to be in the country again illegally, they will be considered category two deportees and forfeit their opportunity to emigrate legally in the future.

If this is not good enough for you the process could be sped up a bit. As the soldiers return from Iraq and Afghanistan they can be redirected to immigration enforcement and the border patrol. More eyes can catch more people crossing the border. More cars can be searched at the checkpoints and more illegals can be rounded up, prosecuted and deported.

More importantly the US can work out a joint coalition with the Mexican government to run the drug cartels out of the border towns. They can arrest the cartel members, protect the public and help to ensure normal legal commerce can exist. This will give the Mexican people less reason to leave their own country if their lives are actually good there.

CHAPTER 3

Welfare Reform

WELFARE REFORM IS another hot button issue. There is great debate over: "What is compassionate support?" and "What is mean-spirited stinginess?". The bottom line I believe is the issue of real need versus fraudulent or unfair use.

In the interests of effectiveness and fairness how do we enact this plan?

First of all, anyone who uses federal support must be a citizen of the United States, pure and simple. Federal funds are collected by the US taxpayer for the use of US citizens and foreigners are not entitled to these funds. So, therefore a Social Security number must be a mandatory piece of identification.

In the case of stolen social security numbers I believe the name and address portion of the social security database should be available to the welfare department offices so that this information can be quickly verified. The agent can look up the number and find out who the federal government issued the number to.

For instance, a person comes up to the welfare signup desk and presents a social security card with a name on it. OK, fine, no problem. The welfare agent punches the number into the system and a totally different name comes up. Problem.

The person insists this is their correct number. The agent can ask the person for his/her address, the person may get this question right. OK. What is the previous address for this person? They probably can't get this one right even if they knew the person's current address.

At this point, the benefits can be denied and the number flagged for investigation if it comes up again. This could be considered a federal crime to deter this from happening in the future.

How much money would this simple change save the government? Welfare would be denied. Food stamps would be denied. WIC funds would be denied. Medicare is denied. Both illegal immigrants and domestic fraudsters would be turned away.

Secondly, the person needs to be truly needy and using their funds for appropriate purposes. This splits into two parts: welfare fraud and substance abuse.

Welfare Fraud: One major move that will reduce fraud is using information systems to make the system more accurate.

A. Debit cards. This is being used already to eliminate the sale of food stamps for cash to use for cigarettes or alcohol. It can also be used to allow only certain items to be purchased. Only staple items of solid nutritional value can be purchased with the cards. In the WIC system there are approved items that can be bought with the vouchers. You may have seen these WIC approved tags on the store shelves. You can buy plain corn flakes but not sugar puffed animal shapes. This can also apply to the food stamp and welfare system as well.

B. Tap into the Global Data Synchronization System. The GDSN system is a global data repository where manufacturers can upload their items' UPC numbers and over 100 other data parameters which can be placed into a database. These parameters can be used to identify items which may be appropriate for use by Food Stamp or WIC recipients. Retailers use this system regularly. The federal government can also download this information and flag items as good or bad. When the UPCs are scanned at the cash register, the purchase will be rejected or accepted immediately saving confusion and paper shuffling in the checkout line.

This can limit purchases not only to eliminate totally inappropriate items but to eliminate its use on high end items and stretch the dollars further. Someone on welfare has no business buying filet mignon or smoked salmon when ground chuck and canned tuna will do just fine. They will pay three or four dollars a pound for meat, not seven or eight.

As with any government program we need to be very careful that they do not use the information for improper means. The government should not be using product information to be the "food police" and tell us what we should eat. Worse yet, they should not implement any taxes or penalties for eating foods the government does not approve of.

Drug Abuse: It is ridiculous to think that the federal government can be giving hundreds of dollars per month to someone who spends at least that much on alcohol or drugs. That is a total waste. Drug testing for all welfare recipients should be mandatory each time they do their quarterly renewal. This will have one of four effects:

1. The person values their welfare payments and will get off the drugs. This person may clean up their act and get a job, thus removing themselves from the welfare rolls and becoming a productive taxpayer.
2. The person values their drugs and gives up the welfare payments. These people most likely will get a job to support their habit if they can, or turn to a life of crime. They may end up in jail and back on the government dole but maybe then that will clean them up.
3. The person quits welfare and struggles to kick the drugs. Eventually they clean up and become productive citizens but bounce back on and off welfare for a while first.

4. The person quits the drugs but never becomes productive. The stay on welfare and remain a drain on our country…. Sad but true. However, time allowed on welfare will have limits.

I believe the first scenario is the most likely. Once people have a clear head they will likely want to do better for themselves. At the very least we won't be paying for their drug abuse. We may need to increase police spending and incarceration costs as a result but hopefully that will only be a temporary situation and in the end, save the country money and probably a lot of lives.

If a person has a valid green card or Visa and finds themselves in dire straits during their stay in the US, some very short term support may be made available as a courtesy to our law abiding neighbors. That is something the legislators would need to debate and develop a criteria and a plan for this.

CHAPTER 4

TAX REFORM

WHO GETS FRUSTRATED with the complex tax returns and the income tax process? Show of hands? I expect that is about everyone, except those with the 1040EZ who don't really need to do anything to fill it out. Americans spend approximately 3 Billion Dollars of time and effort on tax return preparation. Isn't this a tremendous waste of resources?

Protests have been held this year with people screaming about the One Percent ruling America and they are the 99%. I really don't know of any category where 99% of Americans have something in common except that we are all here. Honestly, I do not see a problem with a certain portion of Americans holding a large part of the wealth. That is just the way it is. Their wealth has little to do with the rest of us as long as we stay informed and active and keep on top of abuses. It is not their fault the rest of us do not have a lot of wealth, that's on us.

Most ridiculous is the laughable assertion by the President and others that the rich are not paying their fair share in taxes. 10% of the population pays 80% of the taxes. So what do protesters consider fair? 100%? Nearly half of Americans pay no federal income tax, 47% of Americans to be exact. Is their 0% too high? Is that fair? Any of those people who have children or other deductions get a refund even though they didn't pay anything. Where does that money come from? It either comes from the rich who pay taxes or borrowed from the growing nations who are rapidly starting to kick our butts in the world market.

Looking at our deficits and debt reduction, if you take all of the income from the top few percent as taxes it would not get the job done. So, the middle and lower classes need to start paying in. Also with the largest uses of taxes being Medicaid Social Security and Defense, if we did not make cuts in these programs, it would require gutting almost every other federal program to free up enough money to balance the budget. Obamacare takes this equation in the wrong direction.

Many families with at least two children and an average salary would get a refund in excess of their tax obligation but that is not really a workable model for a sustainable nation. I think a flatter tax rate with everyone paying something is a better route to go. No one should get a refund greater than their contribution. Certainly, receiving federal Welfare payments should be deducted from whatever refund you may be due. We'll have more on the welfare system later.

In any case, a flatter tax will have several benefits:

1. We eliminate most of the $3 Billion spent on tax preparation each year. This money and time could be put to more intelligent uses.

2. Cut the Internal Revenue Service down to a skeleton of what it is now, a huge savings. There will be very few questions about how to fill out the forms, all of which could be handled by a Frequently Asked Questions on their webpage. The department will be down to data processing which could be almost entirely automated or online, and enforcement staff. Customer service could be handled by just a few people for those who can't get to the FAQ page.

One BIG negative unfortunately is the total gutting of the tax preparation and accounting industries as far as tax preparation is concerned. Between the IRS employees and the CPAs who lose their jobs, this is a big shift in employment. The initial savings on the payroll could be reverted to job retraining for the first four years. These folks can train for new careers. After four years they should be ready to move on successfully.

Two proposals made in the somewhat recent past have merits but are probably not what we need at least on the short term.

Proposal #1: Straight Flat tax

Presidential candidate Steve Forbes proposed in 1992 a 17% flat tax for everyone. Now, this will reduce the taxes paid by the rich and balance it with tax contributions from the 47% who currently pay no taxes. Assuming the Forbes camp did the calculations to ensure this will keep the government revenue neutral then it is a fairer system and saves America the three Billion dollars in tax preparation plus the benefits of the slimmed down IRS.

The negatives however is that the 47% who don't pay taxes suddenly lose more than 17% of their income. Under the current system with the tax cuts implemented by the Bush administration in place, that is $1000 per child for the child tax credit alone. This will have a devastating effect on this population if the tax savings by businesses and the wealthy are not passed down to the employees in time to make up the difference with a minimum of 17% pay increase across the board.

Proposal #2: The 9-9-9 plan.

In 2012 Presidential candidate Herman Cain proposed the 9-9-9 plan. This would be a flat income tax of 9 percent for citizens, 9% for corporate profits, and 9% for a consumption or sales tax. This is a better plan for these reasons:

1. It would have less impact on the standard American taxpayer in that their income tax burden would increase to 9% rather than 17% but it still increases nonetheless. Loss of tax credits would be painful for most.

2. Corporations would have a large tax reduction from 36%, one of the highest in the world to only 9%. This will help greatly in bringing jobs back to our shores and allowing companies to invest in facilities onshore providing jobs for many more people here.

3. Sales tax gives people choice in whether or not they pay tax. This will raise the overall tax rate but it is totally voluntary. You can save your money or spend it. You only pay the tax if you spend. This also puts those with high disposable income in a position to shoulder more of the tax burden. Essentially this raises taxes on the rich, however, only if they choose to spend it, which removes this taxation from government control.

However, 9% increase in all consumer goods in addition to existing State sales taxes would have a short term effect of putting the brakes on our economy. It makes all consumer products more expensive and may slow the economy with smaller shopping baskets per trip. However as with any tax change or higher gas prices, we get used to it.

Proposal #3: The Gorman plan.

This plan is similar to the 9-9-9 but a bit of a hybrid with the flat tax including adjustments to make it more workable and palatable to more people. Since elimination of our unconstitutional income tax is not likely my provisions would be like this:

1. A two-tiered federal income tax of 10% for income over the poverty line and 25% for income in excess of 1 million dollars per year. Child tax credits, home mortgage interest deduction and charitable contribution deduction would remain. A middle tier of 15% on earners between $500,000 and one million may be added if this plan will not provide sufficient revenue.

2. Reduce corporate tax rate to15% or less.

3. Federal sales tax of 3%. This would be on any consumer

goods with the exception of regular grocery items, toiletries and basic clothing.

So what are the benefits of this plan?

1. Two tiered format is simple but fair. No one living in the United States and using our infrastructure should be totally free of taxes. This would allow lower rates for those making less money and higher rates for the so called "rich". Other proposed plans raising tax rates for those making in excess of $250,000 hurt the people who are in the prime earning years and taking away incentive to build businesses and achieve big things. $250,000 hits business owners right when they start to pick up steam. Most people can retire on 1 million dollars so if people are making that annually they can afford to give up more of that money.

2. Tax credits for children and home mortgage interest will remain. The two greatest expenses for families are mortgages and child rearing. This will lessen the burden on those who need to keep their income most desperately and their tax burden will be below the 15%.

3. Reduction of the corporate tax rate will allow businesses to compete on a more level playing field in the global marketplace. This is the new world we live in and we need to play the game. 36% corporate tax rate is the highest in the world and is stifling much of our job growth and fueling offshoring of businesses since many of those countries our businesses are expanding to charge single digit tax rates.

4. Sales tax is always seen as something that hurts business and slows growth so it needs to be small. Exempting basic groceries, toiletries and clothing items will make this tax minimal to low income families and the working poor. If most of their spending is on basic necessities they will essentially be tax free. As we said above, the rich will pay the most taxes here

because they have the money to spend. It is a tax increase on the rich only if they choose to spend that portion of their income, which will trickle down to the workers who produce whatever they buy.

What are basic items?

Food: it would be items such as milk and eggs, ground chuck, cheese singles, and standard priced items such as condiments, bread, meat and vegetables, etc., very much like the list used for the WIC food program. More expensive items would be due the tax: higher end brand name items such as gourmet salad dressings, cereals, fancy breads, steaks, smoked salmon, caviar etc.

Toiletries: regular priced soaps, shampoo, toothpaste, deodorant, toilet paper, etc. Each item category will have a maximum allowable price. Items such as makeup and perfume will always be taxed.

Clothing: basic items such as $25 blue jeans, shirts, underwear, shoes or other regular price items would be exempt. Designer jeans, $100 athletic shoes, silk shirts and lingerie would always be taxed. Dress and athletic shoes would have a price limit. Stiletto heels, jewelry or very expensive designer items will always be taxed.

I do not know the complex calculations and criteria involved to calculate the final tally of income that would come as a result of this plan that is a bit over my head. We are looking at the fairness issue and what structure is most equitable assuming the flat tax and 9-9-9 are based on actual economic figuring. The numbers can be adjusted when actual calculations are run. If someone knows those calculations please feel free to send the method and the results and this can be detailed in a later edition.

One question to pose to our legislators... If legally, parents are responsible for their children until age 18 or in some states until they graduate High School, whichever is later, why does the child tax credit expire at age 17? Since taxes are based on the child's status as of December 31st, any child born in December essentially falls off the credit at age 16. I was just wondering what the logic was there, if there was any logic.

Now, we've hearing the news many times about Warren Buffett paying a lower tax rate than his secretary. This also applies to people like Mitt Romney. Don't let them fool you. If you take that one sound bite out of context that sounds shocking but they left out all the important information. First of all, if you look at straight income, Buffett certainly pays a higher tax rate on his salary income than his secretary at 36% but that portion of his salary is very small compared to his investment income. With the Bush tax cuts in place, Buffet would be paying 15% on dividends and 15% on capital gains both of which are below the lowest income tax bracket which is 16%. Also, top notch Administrative Assistants can make in excess of $100,000 so I doubt his secretary is in the 16% bracket and I also doubt she is hurting for money.

Taking this idea further, most Americans these days need to invest their own money for retirement and do not get a pension, so this dividend and capital gains tax cuts affect **everyone** not just the wealthy. Insinuations that these tax cuts are for the wealthy is a bunch of garbage. It very much affects the middle class as much as the wealthy because it affects the amount of your investments that you actually get to use when you liquidate it to useable cash. Middle class folks need every penny they earn while the wealthy may lose more in tax increases but their investments are scaled up to a level that they still have enough to live just fine. The wealthy may gain or lose more money than the middle class but it affects both, just on a different scale.

Other tax issues:

Another big issue related to taxation is duplicate taxes. We need to take some time to compile a listing of these taxes that are redundant and pare them down. Now it is not possible to eliminate every duplication scenario but some are obvious.

The inheritance tax makes little sense. Basically after someone has worked their entire life to put away a nest egg of typically "after tax" money, if the nest egg is big enough, the federal government feels they are entitled to take some of it. Why? The person is simply giving his nest egg to someone else. No commerce has taken place, why does the government deserve to take some. Furthermore, after the "after tax" inheritance is invested then the inheritor will pay additional taxes such as capital gains later on before they can use it.

Here's a funny one, The Gas Guzzler Tax. We already have gasoline taxes paid on every gallon of gas sold. A "gas guzzler" essentially is a car with low gas mileage. So, a person who buys the muscle car or big luxury vehicle will be using more gas and thus paying more tax for every mile they drive. So, in a social engineering move the government decided if we tax these cars up front before the first gallon of gas is bought, maybe these people won't buy the cars in the first place.

That is funny. If you can afford the gasoline and the car and like it enough to pay those costs why would that tax stop you from buying the car you love. From a redundancy standpoint the government is already making higher gasoline tax off of this car. Why double dip and tax the vehicle again? This tax would likely be $3000-$5000 or more on these cars, so it is significant. Also, it is another way the rich are voluntarily paying taxes the middle class and lower are not.

CHAPTER 5

Health Care Reform

THERE IS NOT one big change or magic bullet to fix health care. This is probably one of the more difficult fixes and will require voluntary adjustments from many parties. The Congressional Budget Office released a report in June 2012 indicating that in spite of the new healthcare reform, spending on health care will increase 93% over the next 25 years and will account for 10.4% of GDP in 2037.

The fix will consist of four parts.

1. Tort reform
2. Increased competition in multiple areas
3. Fix of Medicare and Medicaid
4. Use computer technology to cut costs

Tort Reform:

If you ask most doctors the largest single expense they have besides the cost of their office is malpractice insurance. There needs to be more control over scope of what patients can sue for and the amounts so that the cost of malpractice premiums are reduced. This will reduce the doctors' expenses and make it possible for their rates to be lower.

A price cannot be put on a human life but the financial impact of a loss can be quantified. The level of incompetence can be measured and punitive damages assigned. These can be set in concrete numbers. Pain and suffering can be estimated based on the age of the patient and their impact on the plaintiff.

Recently the state of North Carolina had a proposal to limit claims to $250,000. That seems like a very low number for a maximum cap since many people earn over $50,000 a year plus or minus the cost of health care coverage. A young family that loses their breadwinner will not get very far on a quarter million. They could be bankrupt in 3 to 5 years if they attempt to maintain a normal lifestyle and investments such as stocks are not keeping pace. This makes life insurance even more important because this will pay the families of the deceased in the case of malpractice. It is not punitive money but it is security. Life insurance is much cheaper than health insurance and any family without life insurance is being quite irresponsible.

I do not think the jury should have carte blanche to name a number. The judge can put a cap on the award but the past has shown many judges will not impose a cap and allow the jury to do what they will. So we need to set down a range of awards that are possible based on various scenarios. If the judge feels the range does not fit the specific circumstances of the situation, the range can be exceeded. This is one of the reasons in this country; every case has a judge presiding. The defendant is then free to appeal if they believe the judge was wrong in exceeding the range and conversely the plaintiff if the award is too small.

So, if we can save the insurance companies money, they can pass it on to the doctors and they can then pass the savings on to us. The passing on of savings is of course, voluntary but competition generally forces the hand of the greedy in our economy.

Increased competition:

This is where reduced costs to the doctors' suppliers and providers will have its greatest effect. If becoming a doctor is more attractive there will be more doctors. Their schedules will no longer be jam packed and they will compete for patients. Rates will drop and costs charged to the patients and insurance companies will drop also. Managed care systems up to this point have had one major flaw. They restrict the doctor's fees but do nothing to decrease their overhead. Increased competition will have the same effect but without the heavy regulatory hand and top doctors still have the freedom to charge top dollar if they have a patient base willing to pay.

If your doctor's schedule is not jammed full they will have extra time to spend with each patient. They will understand you and your conditions better they will be able to focus longer on your case and make better decisions. The quality of care will improve and overall cost for your care will drop since you will be healthier and less time wasted on tests you don't need.

If you don't feel you doctor is giving you the time and care you need, move on. Go to the doctor down the street. You are in control of your health care and the doctor needs to realize that. Many act like they do not. Go to the next doctor. The old stereotype of long waiting room times and short appointments came about for a reason. If the next doctor's care and rates are to your liking, stay, tell your friends. Soon, the good doctors will have full schedules and the not so good doctors will begin to wonder where everybody went… Not necessarily a bad situation. Good doctors' rates can rise and the bad will need to drop. If the good doctors begin to jam their schedules or overcharge, them the market can correct and patients will flee. This is also not necessarily a bad deal. That is the free market system.

Reduce the cost of malpractice insurance and you open the door to lower rates. What happens to a business if competition forces them to reduce rates to below their cost? They go out of business. Reduce the costs and the possibility for lower rates is real. Malpractice insurance allows doctors to pursue aggressive care without a guarantee of losing their practice but if the cost drives intelligent realistic people of good common sense from the profession, no one wins.

We also need to find ways of having better competition for insurance as well. Keeping insurance private with many providers competing for customers is the best way to do this. Once again if you don't like the service, you can walk. Take your business elsewhere. Premiums too high? Walk. Copays too high? Walk. Coverage stinks? Run!

Many people do not question the costs charged. They do not realize that can shop around for things like surgical services. Surgical clinics and hospitals can charge radically different amounts for the same procedure. A survey of 300 hospitals and clinics showed that the cost of an appendicitis ranged from $1800 to $183,000. Which one would you pay? If everyone shopped around, no one would pay the $183,000 and that facility would need to make some changes or fold.

Also, we need to check to ensure that high costs have been billed correctly. For instance, an insulin pump or pacemaker are expensive to install but much less cost to maintain. There have been cases where maintenance care has been billed under the installation code repeatedly, costing tens of thousands of dollars too much. What do you think this does to your health insurance costs?

Insurance is a business just like any other. It is all about money for them. Many working in the industry are committed to providing quality care but they won't lose their shirts to do it. If your doctor and all the others reduce their rates due to competition and reduced expenses that allows the insurance companies to also reduce their rates and competition improves in that realm as well.

This whole idea of single payer government insurance takes the control of your healthcare out of your hands and into the government's. Competition is out the window and you need to trust the government to make wise decisions on your behalf. Do you trust them to do that with your health?

The government plan Mitt Romney started as Governor of Massachusetts is a better choice, if the government needs to be involved. I don't believe they do but let's explore that option...

The Massachusetts plan requires everyone to purchase health care from some source or suffer a painful monetary fine, this way no one gets free care and hospitals are not left footing the bill for the uninsured (Read: reduced costs to hospitals/ pass on the savings). The plan is graduated based on income. Low income people pay a small premium and get more care than they can afford in the end. Higher income people and those with private health insurance pay much higher rates. These rates are purposely higher than their private plan. So, for them the government plan makes no sense, they are free to purchase the public plan but if they do so, they will overpay and sub-sidize the poor. It remains their choice and the government plan then becomes a part of the competitive mix. If perchance the government plan provides superior service and you are willing to pay for it, then you are free to select that option. Private health insurance can con-tinue to function without being kneecapped by the government plan.

On a Federal level this cannot happen. First off, the federal Government does not have the authority to mandate the purchase of insurance or any product the way the states do, so "Romneycare" was possible, "Obamacare" is not. Medicare is already in place so why add another healthcare plan? The states are free to set up their own plans if they wish. We'll touch more on Obamacare in its own section.

For pharmaceuticals it is more complicated, research and devel-opment are incredibly expensive and the patent holders rightly need to recoup their investment. Those that hold the patent on the drug have a monopoly until the patent runs out. Once that occurs com-petitors are allowed to produce the drug also and generic drugs are reasonably cheap and in that case, after the patent expires, competi-tion is doing its job. The best way to reduce costs of drugs may be to find ways to reduce the cost of R&D. That issue is far beyond the scope of this book and not an area I have much knowledge of anyway.

Fix Medicare and Medicaid:

The whole issue of health care reform hinges on these programs. The only people who should be getting healthcare assistance from the government for the most part are the elderly and the handicapped. We can make exceptions for short term need such as the COBRA program for the temporarily unemployed. I have no issue with these.

Scrapping these programs to replace it with health care program for everyone is ludicrous.

Consider this fact alone. Between 2010 and 2050 the number of people over the age of 65 will double. If these people are retired, they are not paying income and payroll taxes. Who is going to pay the federal health care bills? All able bodied people should be working and paying into the health care plans for the elderly and the handicapped or it will not work. We can't be paying health care for people who are perfectly capable of getting jobs with benefits or buying their own.

This is similar to the problems the auto industry has faced. In 1990 or so when Lee Iacocca retired as chairman from Chrysler the company had more retirees than employees. They could not compete on price with imports when the retiree benefits were such an enormous cost to the company and did nothing to improve the quality of the current product. This is a problem our country is soon to face if we do not make some changes.

For these programs as well as social security, the eligibility age needs to rise along with the average life expectancy and should be permanently tied to that life expectancy. Why? Did you know that when social security age was set at 65, the average life expectancy of the American male was only 62 years old? That means that 100% of Americans would pay into the system and less than 50% of Americans would ever see a dime of Social security. Now the average life expectancy is 78 years so a majority of Americans collect Social Security for 10-15 years. When the population of Americans over 65 doubles we need to be sure the percentage of people paying in remains much higher than those withdrawing money out.

Stories of Medicare fraud are rampant and this also needs to be reined in. The government should consider Medicare fraud an assault on the elderly and the handicapped and punish it severely. How do you feel when you see a thug knock Grandma down for her purse? This is no different except that the thief is kicking you and me too, taking our tax dollars and weakening our nation.

Computer technology:

There is already a push to digitize medical records. Part of this is mandated by the new health care plan but it makes sense for individual doctor's offices to do the same thing anyway to streamline their patient care and billing. A sticky point comes when you talk about centralizing this data for all doctors to access it from one location. This can be a tremendous time and effort savings but the big question is who will own the system, and how will it be controlled?

This idea smacks of Big Brother and much of the argument against it stems from the idea that the government can tax or legislate based on personal medical conditions, etc. You'd like to trust them but as we've seen, not very likely that it will be used entirely on the up and up.

However, let's look at the idea. Have you ever switched doctors and need your medical records transferred? What about being referred to a specialist and the general practitioners findings such as lab results, exams and X-rays need sent across? Then consider the times one of the above was supposed to occur and you showed up for your appointment only to find that there is no information there for the doctor. Even more painful is the time you spent trying to get the info there. Then the time spent by the medical office on each end to **not** get them there. Another scenario, maybe you need information from a doctor you saw ten years ago but he retired and the office is closed. Maybe a central database doesn't sound so bad?

The database will have all of this information in there. You would go online and create a login and password for the specialist or doctor you need to see. This password will only be valid for a number of days which you specify. Then you just e-mail the login info to the doctor you need to see a few days in advance and you are done. That's all the effort needed to get the records over there. After the appointment the doctor will upload the new findings and they are ready for your GP to look over, you can access them anytime you want or send to the next doctor you see later.

This database should be subcontracted to a trusted third party using the state of the art encryption and firewall security. Severe penalties for data breaches or misuse would be imposed. Military engineering and construction is subcontracted, so can this. A key to this situation would be that the government cannot access this database without a warrant specifying specific reasons they need the info and what they plan to do with it. There would be very few if any legitimate reasons for the government to have this information. This falls under illegal search and seizure in the constitution and violating this provision would be a felony.

It may be fine for the government to run generic statistical analysis on the data but that is something the legislature will need to watch and see that it is not used to micromanage people's lives by legislating what you can eat and drink and how we live our lives. There have been far too many government officials of both state and federal meddling in the day to day rights of American citizens. For instance, In New York, Mayor Michael Bloomberg's plan to make sugared soft drinks over 16 ounces illegal for sale. How in the world is this any of the government's business?

Medicare fraud can also be tightened and reined in using computer technology. Computer forensics should be able to tie together patterns of fraud and catch many more offenders.

Obamacare - Patient Protection and Affordable Care Act

If there is any one thing threatening the economic future of our nation as we know it is the

Patient Protection and Affordable Care Act plan railroaded in by Congress....

This plan is obviously set up to put more people on the federal support roles by its structure. That is the opposite of what should be happening at the federal level.

This system requires everyone to buy health insurance, which is not constitutional in the first place. Then the penalty imposed for not buying health care is so small that you would be foolish to buy private coverage. So, what is the effect?

Under this plan, employers would be foolish to offer health care for their employees. Just pay the fine and get on with life with increased profits. Next, the private health insurance companies begin going out of business because few people are buying their services. This will force many people out onto the unemployment lines. Many may find jobs in the federal healthcare system but since a single payer will have less duplication of services than many individual providers, the pool of jobs will drop, leaving many without work.

Now at this point we have a healthcare monopoly. The government can set whatever rates they wish, they can pay for whatever they wish and deny what they wish. The doctors cannot set their own rates because the government can just refuse to pay it and then who can they complain to? Either the patients pay out of pocket or the doctors must take a financial hit.

What recourse do we have? We can't take our business elsewhere because the government is the only provider in town. Maybe they will decide to jack up rates to pay for some other federal program. They have taken money from other programs and put it in the general fund before, who's to say they won't do it with healthcare?

This situation also strikes me as an opportunity for expansion of a medical black market. This occurs in the case of harvesting organs for transplantation and child adoption. Why would it not happen in relation to appendicitis, gall bladder surgery and the similar procedures? This was one reason Roe v. Wade was passed in 1973, to prevent black market abortions. Do we bring this back for medical care in general?

There is great debate about the quality of coverage. Most people who have used government health care in other nations prefer the American system we have now. The government claims there will not be rationing of healthcare. They may not intend to but it WILL happen. How?

Well, the lucrative, fulfilling nature of being a medical practitioner will be ruined. The number of people willing to go to medical school and go through all that it takes to get there will be reduced, since the high income will not be there and the bureaucracy will be increased. Doctors have already been complaining about the managed care bureaucracy for decades. There will be fewer practitioners and many more patients since everyone will now be covered. There will be much longer waits for appointments and procedures, some may be denied for lack of service. Get the picture?

An example: In State sponsored Medicare programs such as TennCare in Tennessee, many doctors will not see patients who are on the plan. The payout for the doctors is too low and they prefer to see patients with the private health insurance. If their schedules still remain full, they have no reason to see the TennCare patients and it is not economically advantageous for them to do so. If there are not private healthcare plans available, the doctors will likely find another line of work such as medical research.

This law also requires states to offer medicare such as this to everyone making less than $30,000 per year. Setting aside the fact that many low income people are that way purely out of their own laziness and have not earned the privilege of good health care. Virginia Governor Bob McDonnell says that would put 400,000 more people on medicare in his state alone. He says they cannot afford that kind of expense. It is an unfunded mandate. Many states are opting out of this plan for the same reason. Virginia has a nice budget surplus of over $100 million and if they can't afford it, then no state with a deficit could possibly afford this plan. So, any state not offering the medicare would force these people into "health care exchanges" on the Federal dime. Then the whole nation has to share the cost. So now the government has given the states incentive to drop out and let people go toward a single payer plan just like the companies dropping their private insurance. Clever!

Will there be the vaunted "death panels" as they are popularly called. These are groups of federal employees who sit and decide whether procedures are appropriate for a person. The name Death Panels comes from opponents of the health care plan based on the example put forth by the President himself. This example was whether or not an elderly woman with cancer would be better off with painkillers and hospice care versus actual cancer treatments. The President felt that in some cases it is best not to treat the woman.

Doctors sometimes do make these calls if a person is a poor candidate for surgery or cannot handle chemotherapy; however this is done with a firsthand knowledge of that person, their total health history and treatment history for this and other conditions. That makes sense; a panel of disconnected bureaucrats cannot accurately make these calls and should not be allowed to.

Another debate has been whether healthcare is a right or a privilege. I do not believe that anyone has a right to health care. Point this out in the Constitution for me, will you? This is another area where this plan will damage our economy and way of life. Growing up, it was a great motivator to work hard and do well in school, so that we can get a "good" job. What is a good job? That is a job with a high income and healthcare plan. What happens if healthcare is provided for everyone? One of the great motivators to work hard and achieve is gone! One of the great drawing cards to work for good companies is their healthcare plan. That competitive advantage to these good corporations is also gone!

So now your motivation to work hard and achieve boils down to how many toys you want to buy. How big of a house do you want? Do you want to eat out or buy cheaper food and cook at home? Many people can stand a drop in salary or a change in careers where income has room to fluctuate. We may change to a more enjoyable, less critical or stressful job when our incomes allow. The one big thing that keeps us working for retail companies, tire manufacturers, steel mills, utilities, sewer maintenance and other important jobs is.....Health Care!

Most appalling in this is that the plan was passed without any serious debate. House Speaker Nancy Pelosi said, "We need to pass it to see what's in it". Excuse me?!! Do you sign your mortgage papers or car loans before you find out the interest rate and term? No! You'd be an idiot to do that. Amazingly, our federal government thinks it is perfectly fine to push through an incredibly expensive piece of legislation without knowing the impact it will have on our nation or even what is in it!

President Obama said in his campaign that we would have transparency and that legislation would be posted for the whole nation to see before Congress had a chance to vote on it. Why did this not happen with the healthcare plan? Why did they complete the legislation and vote on it four hours later? Why was this legislation not posted on the website in PDF format where it could be downloaded and searched by keywords so people could find the topics they were most interested in? Why did they vote on this legislation without a report from the Congressional Budget Office to tell us what this was going to cost the nation? Based on CBO estimates, Obamacare's overall 10-year costs would likely eclipse $1.9 trillion not the 938 billion advertised.

With the amazing technology we have today, a law should be passed where all bills are posted on the website for a period of time so that everyone has a chance to read it and let their opinions be known to their legislators. This way we don't have a majority of people objecting to a bill that is already law and fighting in the courts to get it repealed. The Healthcare plan should never have made it to the President's desk for a signature. Once the people read it and contacted their legislators with their opinions, it would have died on the House floor. This is not what the founding fathers set up for us; this is not how America works.

It is sad that the Supreme Court upheld the constitutionality of Obamacare since it is clearly unconstitutional. The vote was 5-4 with Chief Justice John Roberts, the tie breaking vote. It is still up to the Congress and Senate to decide if the law remains in place.

The Department of Health and Human Services cites three constitutional provisions with authority for the mandate — the Taxing Power, the Commerce Clause, and the Necessary and Proper Clause.

The Cato Institute makes their case against the constitutionality of the law as follows:

1. The penalty for not buying health insurance is not a tax. Even if the penalty were a tax, it would fail the constitutional requirements for income, excise, or direct taxes.

2. The power to regulate interstate commerce extends only to economic activities; it does not permit Congress to compel such activities in order to regulate them.
3. The mandate is not necessary; it is a means to circumvent problems that would not exist if not for the law itself. The mandate is also not within the scope of the original founding father's idea of limited federal government.

Additionally, in 2014 health care billing code list will be expanded from 13,000 codes to 144, 000. What do you think this will do to the accuracy of health insurance billing? There will be many procedures overbilled just for lack of familiarity by the billing staff. If you were unsure and had the option of making a mistake bringing your employer extra money or less which code would you pick?

"The nine most terrifying words in the English language are 'I'm from the government and I'm here to help.' " – Ronald Reagan

CHAPTER 6

Energy

THE FEDERAL GOVERNMENT keeps pushing clean renewable energy such as solar and wind power but is that the best choice for our nation? These energy sources are wonderful in that they are plentiful and won't go away but are obviously not ready for primetime. Who wants windmill fields ruining the landscape? Solar companies such as Solyndra continue to go out of business.

If these clean energies are so important and so good for us, why is there not a solar array and a windmill on the roof of every federal building? That is a great indicator of how much the Feds actually believe in the technology. Why give Solyndra 500 million dollars in stimulus money and watch it go out of business when a government contract to supply panels to all government buildings would have been a win-win for everybody.

Ethanol has been a loser. It is expensive to produce, hard to transport, saves nothing to the consumer at the pump. Ethanol production has depleted corn reserves and made corn products and animal feed more expensive. Thus, meat is more expensive. Oil is easily transported by pipeline, ethanol cannot be. Oil is pushed through the pipes with high pressure water and the oil and water natural separate at the end. Alcohol and water mix and would need to be distilled at the end of the pipeline, so truck or train transport is the only possibility. Those vehicles burn diesel fuel so how is that saving on oil?

Furthermore, I remember in the early 1990s bakeries being upset that the federal government was requiring smokestack scrubbers because the alcohol burning out of the bread was causing ground level ozone. Then they started requiring ethanol added to gasoline to **reduce** ozone. Huh? Does that make any sense or have I misunderstood the chemistry here?

Until these technologies finally grow up, the clear winner in the clean fuel wars is Natural Gas. With recent discoveries of natural gas, the prices are now at record lows in contrast to gasoline which is staying very high, as we all know.

A 2007 report of the Potential Gas Committee of the Colorado School of Mines determined that in 2006 the U.S. had a natural gas resource base of 1,525 Trillion cubic feet of natural in the U.S. (about an 82 year supply). When you count the methane hydrates compressed under the ice caps which we currently do not have the technology to extract and under the tundra in the northern hemisphere, it is estimated there could be 200,000 Trillion cubic feet or close to 9,000 years of supply at current U.S. consumption levels. Even if we convert all vehicles to natural gas power I assume the natural gas supply would probably still last longer than humans have been on the earth to this point.

According to the EPA, in comparison to a coal-fired power plant, natural gas produces half as much carbon dioxide, less than a third as much nitrogen oxides, and one percent as much sulfur oxides.

Natural Gas combustion does not produce any solid waste or polluted water discharge that needs to be disposed of. If the gas is being used to heat water in a boiler that water needs dealt with but water is not necessary to use natural gas.

Plus, the process of extraction and transport of the natural gas generates fewer emissions. Who ever heard of a natural gas spill? Methane gas would simply float away as long as it was not in a confined space or in enough concentration to cause explosion. Methane is more damaging to the atmosphere than carbon dioxide but that is only in its raw form. Burning natural gas converts it into carbon dioxide which, when you think about it, makes it cleaner than where it started. As we said the CO2 emission levels are much lower than what comes from gasoline or coal combustion.

So, hey, maybe we should put spark plugs in our undershorts for those times where we have the big bean burrito? Do it for the environment. Diaper the cows. Eat mor Chikn.

According to a Discoverynews.com article, US automakers are working toward natural gas vehicles which are already in mass production by Honda. The biggest drawback to the vehicles is that the fuel tanks are large compared to equivalent gasoline tanks, limiting the amount of fuel the vehicle can carry and the number of refueling stations are minimal with around 400 nationwide. Vehicles need to travel within close range of the stations. Work is being done to make smaller fuel tanks that can hold more fuel providing greater range.

There are two types of natural gas fuel:

1. Compressed natural gas (CNG) is pressurized gas stored in a similar way to a vehicle's gasoline tank.
2. Liquefied natural gas (LNG) is produced by chilling natural gas to about minus 260 degrees Fahrenheit. This essentially compresses the gas to a smaller volume in the chilling process.

Synthetic motor oils are made from hydrogenating methane gas to make it a liquid, similar to how liquid vegetable oil is turned into solid margarine. The thickness of the oil is determined by how long you hydrogenate it rather than adding plastic polymers as with petroleum oil. The plastic polymers break down with heat and turn to varnish. This is one of the reasons synthetic oils are superior. Now, hopefully the abundance of natural gas will make the synthetic oils cheaper.

Sergio Marchionne, the chief executive of Fiat and Chrysler, says natural gas has greater potential than electricity to power vehicles. In early March 2012, Chrysler unveiled a pick-up truck than can use liquefied natural gas and went on sale in June. General Motors makes two vans that use compressed natural gas, the Chevy Express and the

GMC Savannah, of which over 1200 have already been sold as fleet vehicles and soon two CNG fueled pick-up trucks will begin production by the end of 2012. Fleet vehicles are prime candidates for using natural gas since they can all fill up at their central facility. This is not a new idea. In the 1978 gas crunch my hometown powered their police cruisers on propane.

Chrysler does not plan to have a passenger car powered by CNG until 2017 while Honda currently sells over 2000 per year across all 50 states, *right now*! In Brazil, the Fiat Sienna Tetrafuel is a true flex fuel vehicle running on gasoline, ethanol or Natural gas. It has auxiliary tanks in the trunk to hold the natural gas fuel. Even in Iran, where gasoline is 15 cents per gallon they sold 500,000 Iran Khodro model CNG powered cars in only two years.

With popularity will come more fueling stations. It would be great if the federal government could give tax breaks to businesses for adding Natural Gas pumps just like they do rebates for the hybrid and electric vehicles. In addition, the cost of retrofitting a regular gasoline vehicle to natural gas operation is far cheaper than designing a hybrid electric vehicle.

This is also a far better idea than the ridiculously wasteful Cash for Clunkers deal in 2009. How many cheap, inexpensive driveable vehicles were destroyed that could have easily been retrofitted to natural gas for less than the price of the federal rebate. These could have been inexpensive vehicles that low income families could have purchased very cheaply. Now the supply of those older inexpensive cars is unnecessarily reduced, hurting the working poor. Obviously helping the poor and the environment were not high priorities for the administration in this deal. It was a quick easy political capital grab.

In order to deal with the low availability of filling stations the traded-in "Clunkers" could all be taken to several locations with high population and poor air quality. Filling stations could be paid to install CNG or LNG pumps at their facilities and trained to maintain and repair the natural gas vehicles. The cars would be sold cheaply to residents in the nearby areas for a small profit to the government.

This would achieve five goals:

1. cleaner air in the polluted areas
2. lower gasoline consumption and fewer oil imports.
3. Cheap reliable transportation to low income people with plentiful filling stations nearby.
4. A shot in the arm for rapid implementation of natural gas as a viable fuel for the general public.
5. The vehicles would be revived and given new life rather than being scrapped and wasted.

How many people in the automotive world would have loved to have those Chevy, Ford and Chrysler V8s and V6s that were destroyed by filling them with liquid glass?

The above being said, who would be opposed to natural gas fuel and why would they be? The only reasons I can see would be that they make money off of other fuels or have a political reason to support something else.

Cap and trade

President Obama said during his campaign for election in 2008 that the Cap and Trade plan would "necessarily bankrupt" businesses who choose to burn coal by levying fines that make it fiscally unsound to do so. That's great for building jobs and supporting the economy isn't it? How much would it cost these companies to convert over to natural gas fuel? Why not give these companies a tax break to encourage natural gas conversions. Is the government's aversion to fossil fuels too strong?

One problem here is that foreign nations will continue to use coal because it is cheap and plentiful. They will even buy the high sulfur coal we won't use because it is even cheaper. It is very damaging to the environment with sulfuric acid raining down from the sky. Meteorologists say that the coal smoke rising into the Jetstream over China is coming to the US and causing a reduction in snowfall in the

Rocky Mountains. This is a huge issue for the water supplies in many western states.

How much good will all of this investment in revamping our businesses' fuel sources do anyway?

According to the Heritage foundation: "The $1.9 trillion of tax revenue generated over eight years from a cap-and-trade bill would .... amount to a nearly $2,000 tax every year for every American household. Projected job losses that would have resulted from the Lieberman-Warner cap and trade would have surpassed 900,000 in some years."

Environmental Protection Agency, says that a 60 percent reduction in carbon-dioxide emissions by 2050 will reduce global temperature by 0.1 to 0.2 degrees Celsius by 2095. So, essentially, the huge effort to reduce carbon dioxide emissions costing billions of dollars in effort and added regulation for the American economy produces virtually no environmental benefit.

Not to say there is or isn't global warming, the greenhouse effect is natural and normal and is what prevents the earth from being an ice ball but global warming proponents have been consistently wrong in their predictions:

To paraphrase Economist Walter Williams: In 1939, the U.S. Department of the Interior said American oil supplies would last only 13 years. In 1949, the Secretary of the Interior said the end of U.S. oil supplies was in sight. In 1974, the U.S. Geological Survey said that the U.S. had only a 10-year supply of natural gas. According to the American Gas Association, (apparently before the recent huge gas discoveries) there's a 1,000 to 2,500 year supply.

Some NASA scientists have also pointed out that global warming models tend to forget about precipitation which has a huge effect on temperature and is wholly unpredictable. That's one of the reasons you can't trust a ten-day weather forecast much less a ten year prediction of global temperatures. This also points to the fact that there is NOT a consensus amongst scientists on the global warming issue. Never mind the widely reported alleged fraud by the NOAA and other organizations that occurred in fudging the global warming data.

Yes, temperatures have been very warm over the past decade but weather is cyclical. It has warm periods and cold periods then it warms back up again. One century of data cannot tell the whole story. How is it also, that as we clean up our environment year after year, the temperature keeps rising? Didn't they tell us in the 1970s that we were headed for a new ice age? It was reported in the 1990's that Greenland had dropped to the temperatures that they believe were present at the start of the ice age. Recently it was reported that Greenland ice was melting over the entire Island. They went on to say that the amount of melting increases and decreases periodically but 100% of the island was unusual. We should watch to see if it swings back the other way again.

Temperatures rose for several centuries until around 1000 AD when they began to drop again. NASA defines the "Little Ice Age" as a cold period between 1550 AD and 1850 AD with three very cold intervals: one beginning about 1650, another about 1770 (remember the stories of George Washington at Valley Forge?), and the last in 1850, each separated by intervals of slight warming.

Proposed causes for these cycles include: cyclical lows in solar activity, higher volcanic activity, changing ocean currents and even fluctuations in human population.

In 1816 there was a "Year without a Summer" after a volcano named Tambora exploded in Indonesia, killing 12,000 people instantly and shading the entire earth and causing dark cold days for a year. Savannah, Georgia recorded their high temperature for the year on July 4th at 46 degrees Fahrenheit. Quebec had a foot of snow in June, and Pennsylvania lakes were frozen until August. During that time the bleakness was reflected in Mary Shelley's story "Frankenstein", which was written during that cold summer when the Shelley's typical summer vacation was ruined by the cold. Swimming and boating were replaced with storytelling.

One sizeable volcanic explosion today and we could see a dramatic reduction in worldwide temperatures causing snow to fall for extended periods, ruining crops, the polar ice caps would accumulate ice and a drop in the ocean levels would result. Would this reverse the warming trend and cause another cooling cycle? It would be interesting to see.

By the way, according to National Geographic magazine August 2009, there is a very large volcano under the plates near Yellowstone National Park which has erupted several dozen times over the past millennia, though not in exactly the same place. The location shifts due to the movement of the plates and the gap in a lower plate which releases the magma is moving westward. This volcano is one of the largest on earth and the last eruption 640,000 years ago was estimated to be 1000 times larger than the Mount St Helens eruption of 1980 and 50 times larger than Krakatoa in 1883. If it erupted again today it could spew ash as far as Texas and cause a huge crater possibly the size of Rhode Island as the earth's crust falls into the hole vacated by the eruption. With the volcanic activity around the "Ring of Fire" in the Pacific region causing earthquakes and tsunamis these past few years, who knows where the next big bang might occur? An explosion in Yellowstone would cause a volcanic winter possibly lasting several years.

CHAPTER 7

Give business back to the businesses

ANY FREE SYSTEM is open to abuse and corruption by the unscrupulous. This is no different for Congress than it is for business owners. So there is a need for regulations to protect consumers other businesses and the environment. However the federal government has gone too far and in many respects has abused their power to overregulate our economy.

It has been said that the Sarbanes-Oxley and Dodd-Frank bills are redundant in a sense, rehashing laws already on the books that if they individually were enforced, neither bill would be necessary. This is a flaw in government oversight that needs to be corrected. The government needs to keep better track of what is already on the books and quit wasting time and money creating new laws and regulations that cost companies millions unnecessarily.

The primary tool used to get the federal government's hands into everything is the Commerce Clause of the US Constitution, Section 8 of article 1. The constitution states that anything not covered in the Constitution is the jurisdiction of the states and the states' right to regulate. The loophole of the Commerce Clause is used is used to touch everything they want to meddle in. All the feds need to do is prove that the business deals in interstate commerce and they can regulate it.

An extreme example is the "Ollie's Barbecue" case **Katzenbach v. McClung in 1964**. In that case the Federal government was attempting to crack down on racial discrimination because the restaurant did not want to serve colored people. The Feds couldn't touch them because it was a private business but they cited interstate commerce as their "IN". The business owner claimed he did not participate in Interstate commerce since all of his food suppliers and customers were local. However, the condiments he used were made out of state and shipped to the local supplier, so they were able to prevent the restaurant from excluding customers based on race.

If the government can get to the nitty-gritty level of what condiments a restaurant uses, as their foot in the door to claim interstate commerce, what business is immune to Federal regulation? The founding fathers did not intend for this to occur, they only wanted to prevent disruptive competition between the states impinging on free commerce such as charging different prices or tariffs on similar items sold across state lines. For instance a local soda pop produced in New York and a similar product in Pennsylvania should be sold equally in each state. One state cannot charge a 50% tariff on imports from the other state and jack up the price of the out of state drink to levels no one would pay. This was the intent of the commerce clause, not as a pry bar to get their dirty fingers into everything.

Some government regulations make no sense and we all have examples of these. Send me your list. Recent events such as the government shutdown of Gibson Guitars go beyond the limits of sensibility. In a time where jobs are scarce and American products are expensive compared to foreign made products, the government shuts down a Tennessee factory because they did not go through the proper procedure in using Rosewood produced in Madagascar. This law only protects the workers in Madagascar while Americans suffer for lost work.

Making the situation worse, it was based originally on a regulation passed in the early 1900s regulating the import of foreign products. This regulation never affected the guitar industry for 90 years. This regulation was updated in 2009 by the Obama administration making the regulations more restrictive. The law states that certain wood products must be finished in the source country before exporting to the United States. This would force Gibson to invest in a facility overseas to finish their wood parts to customer specifications before shipment or close their Memphis plant and make all of their guitars overseas. So, another business would be outsourced solely because of federal regulation made by our own government. How is that for boosting the economy?

The Gibson guitar factory was raided later in 2009 and all of their Rosewood seized. Charges were never filed and the wood was not returned to the company. Again in 2011 the Gibson factory was raided, the Rosewood was seized, this time the factory was shut down temporarily but again, the wood was not returned and no charges have been filed. Why? Gibson continues to produce their famous Gibson USA Les Paul guitars in Memphis but without the Rosewood option which is a favorite of many guitar players. Rosewood is better than maple but much less expensive that Ebony which would be another imported wood and potentially suffers the same problem. This seriously affects their competitiveness against rival guitar makers and was essentially pointless.

Administrative Law:

The founding fathers in their wisdom set up an interesting aspect of our government that allows for additional flexibility in addition to the three houses set up in Articles 1 through 3. To some extent it could be considered a fourth section of the government. However they left too much flexibility and power in this area and trusted that their successors would have similar wisdom. That is rarely the case.

This area is Administrative Law for which the Constitution gives every President the power to create. For example the Department of Homeland Security, Department of Education, the Environmental Protection Agency, and so forth.

This is a good idea in theory but only if the legislators and the participants in each administration are trustworthy. This has become a runaway freight train of sorts crashing across the American way of life. The foxes are watching the henhouse while the horses have left the barn. This area needs to be revamped to put checks and balances within the administrative system.

Keep in mind that a person or business found in violation of administrative regulations cannot appeal their case to federal court until **all** administrative avenues have been exhausted within that Administration. This is particularly difficult when you realize that the administration itself is the rule makers, inspectors, prosecutors, investigators, litigators, judges and levier of punishment in the administrative system. There is no direct outside influence on the decisions of the administration except possibly urgings from the President. If the administration decides it wants to punish someone, it can then skew the entire process in their favor by issuing instructions down the chain of command. Until the punishment is levied and the case closed, the defendant cannot appeal to the outside courts for assistance. Thankfully, that is an option if the administration abuses its power, but it is a long, frustrating and expensive way down the road in this process.....Just ask the folks at Gibson.

My solution to the administrative Law monopoly:

1. The administration will remain free to make is rules and regulations as it wishes.
2. The inspectors will remain within the administration to spot violators.
3. Investigators will be reassigned to a new Administrative Law division of the FBI. We already have an investigative body, let's use it. This will not increase the number of federal employees, just change who they answer to. The investigators will answer to the Head of Administrative Investigation who answers to the FBI director.
4. Litigators and judges will be relocated to the Department of Justice. These will answer to the Attorney General's office.

In this process, the same FBI investigators and Justice Department litigators will work with all administrative departments equally, avoiding any favoritism.

So, once a violation is found, the inspectors will forward their report to the Justice Department who will decide if the violation is worth anyone's time.

If the violation is seen to be legitimate it will be sent to the FBI who will investigate the allegations and send their findings to the defendant, Administration and the Justice department.

If the FBI feels there is no violation, the case is closed. If the violation is confirmed, the justice department can prosecute the case in Administrative Court.

One point of genius in the constitution is that Federal judges are appointed for life. They are immune to being fired or voted out except in case of severe misconduct. A bad judge could still be a problem in that case but thankfully, the presidential administration and the Department of Justice have no power of influence on the judge. There are no campaign contributions or threats that can affect the judge's job or decisions, especially in the case of judges appointed by previous presidential administrations.

This process will reduce the number of frivolous or unnecessary litigations by letting impartial third parties intervene early in the process. American business can operate in less fear of the big foot of the government.

The results of the case will be posted on a website dedicated to this purpose for the entire world to see. The violation, evidence, argument and verdict will be available for public review and to either concur or express their outrage, creating transparency as President Obama promised.

In the end many of these administrations probably need to be eliminated due to either redundancy or just are not very useful. For example the Department of Homeland Security is a total waste except as a great political grandstanding move. We already have the FBI for internal investigations and the CIA for action outside of our country.

The National Transportation Safety Board already exists. Do we really think that airlines are going to let terrorists on their airplanes if we let them police their own security? Exploding planes are very bad for business. The airline also will not want to alienate customers so will find much more user friendly ways of doing security checks for fear of losing revenue to the competition.

CHAPTER 8

United States Sovereignty

UNITED STATES SOVEREIGNTY. What's that? Basically that is the state of being where the United States is its own independent nation in control of its own policies and laws.

OK, so what is the problem here? The problem is that slowly but surely our government is giving this away. We are relinquishing authority to the United Nations. We are taking global laws and policies as our own.

An example of loss of sovereignty is the Euro currency. Most of Europe gave up their sovereignty over their economies by changing to the Euro. Now many of those are regretting the decision. The United Kingdom has retained control over their currency much to the protest of the European Union but it is not the EU's call to make. The UK has retained their economic control over the Pound.

Now countries need to be bailed out for not taking care of their own economies and the EU is considering making them return to their own independent currency so they are not dragging down the others in the Union. So apparently those who need to contribute to the bailout don't think this EU is such a good idea now, do they?

There have been proposals that the United States, Mexico and Canada create their own economic Union. Do we really want that? Aside from oil, sports, vacations and beer what do we really need from either of these countries? We can buy and sell products across the borders freely. That is fine.

One of the best ideas maybe to run an oil pipeline from the Canadian oil fields to the Gulf of Mexico. Oh wait we just tried that. It was blocked by the US government. Mexico and Canada are our biggest suppliers of non-domestic oil, not OPEC so we do need to protect that relationship.

Mexican trucks have been allowed to run up and down the roads of the US and at times have been deemed unsafe. If they want to run on our roads they should be forced to have annual inspections at a US facility to ensure the brakes, tires and other safety parts are up to standard. They also should not allow badly maintained oil belching machines to smog up our air either.

What about these G8 summits and other gatherings where countries get together to decide global environmental policies for the group? This could be good discussion to get everyone on the same page. Cooperation can be beneficial but we need to be cognizant of giving away too much control over our own environmental policy.

A major threat is a treaty called "Constitution for the Oceans". This was put together over a 9 year period in the 1970s and completed during the Carter administration. The treaty was rejected in 1982 by the Reagan administration and may have been ratified had Jimmy Carter won reelection. 119 counties originally signed this treaty on December 10, 1982 and now 150 have put pen to this document, which has been described by the "International Foundation for the Law of the Sea" as "a compulsory legal order for all oceans, including the seabed and deep seabed. Its regime encompasses all uses of the ocean space, from shipping to fisheries and from ocean mining to energy extraction." This treaty has been revived by the Obama administration and stands chance of being passed by the end of 2012. Watch the lame duck Congress. There also is a provision where a certain portion of all oil sales from the deep sea worldwide will be put into an international fund and given to poor third world countries. This is yet another plan for income redistribution sending American money to foreign nations.

Another threat already in action in the US is a policy called

"Agenda 21" which may be the single biggest blow to our sovereignty to date. This plan is an international guide for how cities and states should be run, how waste should be dealt with and how the environment should be protected. This is a product of the United Nations Conference on Environment and Development (UNCED) held in Rio de Janeiro, Brazil, in 1992 and is an action plan of the United Nations related to sustainable development. This was ratified by 178 governments on that date including the United States under President George HW Bush, during a two week conference capping three years of work drafting the plan. President Clinton followed up in 1995 with Executive Order #12858, creating a Presidential Council on 'Sustainable Development.'

President Obama has also signed Executive Order 13547 creating the National Ocean Council which is to develop "coastal and marine spatial plans" to "ensure the protection, maintenance, and restoration of the health of ocean, coastal, and Great Lakes ecosystems and resources". This is passed under the auspices of Agenda 21 but sounds strikingly similar to the Constitution for the Oceans does it not?

Criticism of Agenda 21 is that private property ownership, private vehicle usage and ownership of private farms may be at risk due to the provisions of Agenda 21.

There are 40 chapters in the Agenda 21, divided into four main sections.

Section I: Social and Economic Dimensions:

This section deals with combating poverty, changing consumption patterns, promoting health, change population and sustainable settlement in decision making.

Section II: Conservation and Management of Resources for Development

Deals with biodiversity, protection of the atmosphere and fragile environments, deforestation, control of pollution and management of biological and radioactive wastes.

Section III: Strengthening the Role of Major Groups:

This describes the roles of women, children and youth, local authorities, businesses and workers communities and farmers also strengthening the role of indigenous peoples.

Section IV: Means of Implementation:

Implementation includes science, technology transfer, education, international institutions and financial mechanisms.

This will seriously limit a local government's ability to make its own decisions. If you think the Federal government is too big for its britches do we want the rest of the world telling your town how to set up its recycling policy or the roles of women and children?

The state of Alabama passed a resolution opposing Agenda 21 and the Republican National Convention has also spoken out in opposition.

Debt....

Don't forget our national debt. This is a scary thing as far as our sovereignty is concerned. It is estimated that the US owes 1.2 billion dollars to China. China has been building their infrastructure, stockpiling resources such as gold, oil, coal and US dollars. As we buy Chinese made products and then pay them interest on the debt, the situation worsens. Our government continues to enact policies that devalue our dollar. We owe 16 trillion dollars in total debt and growing fast. If China calls in their 1.2 trillion, what would we do? This is approximately $15,000 per American household. What if everyone called in their debt? At 16 trillion dollars, this would be approximately $51,000 for each person in the United States. Multiply this by the number of people in your household and this is your family's share.

I hope Congress has an answer.

CHAPTER 9

Moral Decay

THE MORAL DECAY of our culture cannot be underestimated in its impact on the current state of the United States of America. What has become of our family structure, our moral values, our pride, patriotism, the economy, work ethic, care for others.... you name it? No prayer in schools since the 1960s, now no Pledge of Allegiance any more either. Do we now remove God from our government documents? These are the kind of silly ideas we are letting happen.

It has been said again and again that you cannot legislate morality. Whether it is or isn't possible is one issue. The fact that the constitution did not name that as one of our governmental responsibilities is another. That leaves it up to the people to police themselves. We need to hold ourselves, our children, friends, neighbors and anyone else we encounter accountable. Do not allow immorality or evil of any kind to exist around yourself or your children. Evil wins when good people do nothing. The good people need to do a lot more.

Granted, at many times in history there have been worse periods for one area or another. Medieval times were not the best for personal security, racism in the 19th and early 20th centuries is downright embarrassing, just for a few examples. What is most disturbing is that in the past 50 years, as society has improved in many areas, American citizens have consciously chosen to forgo basic moral values and ethics. We have gotten so comfortable with our security and prosperity that we feel free to do as we wish. We think that the rules of conduct are not important anymore and that as long as we are sufficiently entertained or that things are done in the name of entertainment, not necessarily in the "real world", that it is OK.

One thing that bugs me is the fallacy of the separation of church and state. The constitution states that the government cannot abridge the freedom to practice religion and they cannot establish a state religion similar to the Church of England. To prohibit nativity scenes, menorah displays in public places and prayer in school, is a violation of the constitution in my mind. If a student wants to say a prayer at their high school graduation the have that right. Schools should provide a moment of silence where each child can pray as they wish. Not to mention the Pledge of Allegiance to the United States which many schools have eliminated. This should be mandatory in all government funded schools. Don't bite the hand that feeds.

Take family structure for example. 20 years ago the big news was the divorce rate exceeding 50%. Now many younger people don't even bother to get married. In 2012, 40% of children are born to single mothers. Does this mean the fathers are not around, unknown, have left, or are living with the mother while retaining the right to leave at any time? What is the intent here? Why is there no commitment, if not to the mother but at least the child? Why would the mothers permit this to occur to her children? Why are people having children without a previous solid commitment that would keep two parents in the home for the duration of the child's upbringing? Teenagers need to be taught better and better supervised to prevent this trend. Parents are really dropping the ball here.

Welfare benefits contribute greatly to that scenario allowing single mothers benefits they would not be entitled to if they were married. Many realize they will have less free money if they get married. This needs to be revised as part of welfare reform. If people can't keep themselves under control or respect moral values, the government should not be enabling them continue the behavior. They should fear an undesirable scenario, not benefit from it. Do we need to take care of people who purposely put themselves in the situation? Certainly we do not. Even without government assistance it is their responsibility to ensure their children do not suffer for the parents mistakes.

Definition of Marriage:

A subject I initially did not include due to the recent controversy on the subject but I have not heard any of the pundits get off their partisan soapbox long enough to look at this logically so here it goes:

There are two issues at work here when you talk about the definition of marriage and the legalization of gay marriage, one religious and one legal and not to be confused.

1. <u>What is marriage?</u> - Marriage at its core is a religious creation or sacrament and nothing else. The definition of marriage comes from the Bible, Torah, Koran or other religious text and nowhere else. It is the joining of a man and woman for the purposes of creating a family which biologically requires one man and one woman. This is a religious issue and the government or the courts have no jurisdiction to change it. This does not relate to legal benefits or property rights.
2. <u>Civil Union</u> - Sometimes referred to as "marriage" and is solely in the control of the states with the issuance of a marriage license. This is done for the legal rights normally associated with marriage, health benefits, social security; property rights etc. and is typically connected to the religious marriage as a package deal. The federal government has no jurisdiction here.

So, what is the bottom line? Marriage is a religious issue; rights to benefits and property etc are a legal issue and are two different conversations. States can pass any laws they wish with regard to what union between people can receive health benefits or property and other issues associated with marriage but they cannot change the definition of what a marriage is. I wish the two issues would not have become so confused.

Essentially "gay marriage" is an oxymoron. They can have their civil unions if their state decides to grant it but it is not a "marriage". The federal government needs to stay out of the conversation; they have no dog in the fight.

Abortion:

Time and time again the "abortion debate" is brought up. I do not understand why there even is a debate. This is a black and white issue. There is no gray area. Abortion is the killing of an unborn child. Why is this an option except in grave medical crisis where it is the only choice to save the life of the mother? The issue of rape and incest is something the legislature will need to take up and decide. It is still a human child in any case.

If you are not sure about that, I have a little experiment that would put this issue to bed once and for all:

1. Take a family that has multiple children and have one of the mother's eggs artificially inseminated from the same father.
2. As soon as that cell splits into multiple cells, mere minutes or hours later, take a DNA sample.
3. Then, take DNA samples from the older children.
4. Submit all three DNA profiles to an independent lab for analysis.
5. Given no information except the DNA profile, ask these doctors to describe each child in detail, hair color, eye color, sex, and other characteristics as well as the ages of the three children.

Now, you can't tell a child's age from a DNA profiles since DNA does not change with age. You will get equally detailed description of all three children. Ask that doctor which one of the three is the zygote which was fertilized mere hours ago, which one is the toddler and which is in elementary school. The doctor will have no idea which is which. There will be no discernible difference between the hours old zygote and the 6 year old.

So then I ask..... Based on the DNA profile, which one is OK to kill? Which one is not yet a human baby? Why is this legal?

Is this an issue of a woman having choice over what she does with her body? Certainly not. It is not her body being destroyed; it is someone else's... at her request.

Mother Theresa the great missionary once said: "It is a poverty that a child should die so that one can live their life the way they choose." This decision to have a child needs to be made before engaging in sexual activity with the knowledge that this is a possibility and accept it. Have a plan to deal with it beforehand. You must live with the results not change your mind after.

Media exposure:

What has happened to the media which we watch or listen to? Shock value sells and everyone trying to upstage the last has raised the level of the average broadcast to intolerable levels of language and immorality.

As late as the early 1980's there was still some respect for the "Family Hour" there was still an hour or two after dinner and before the children's bedtime where you could count on the television to be clean. From 7:00 to 9:00 children could watch TV and not be exposed to language or sex. That is all out the window now. Cable channels are not broadcast over the air so are not regulated by the FCC. Now most channels are cable only, even the networks don't see a reason to keep their broadcasts clean if they want to compete. It has been an unlevel playing field with broadcast networks ability to push the envelope restrained by FCC regulation.

Even your typical sitcom is written to appeal to young adults or teens who like sexual situations or bad language. Children are exposed to these at a ridiculously young age and the argument is made that they hear it in school anyway so it isn't a problem. We need to reverse the trend and move this out of the hours where children watch so that once they stop seeing it on TV, eventually younger children will not see it at school and the age of exposure will progressively rise up again to later and later. It may be wishful thinking at this stage but you CAN choose not to watch these shows. Write to the network and advertisers and tell them to find another customer.

The so called "reality TV" on cable channels and daytime tabloid talk shows are the worst and most prolific offenders. The networks take the worst of what America has to offer and broadcast it world-wide for everyone to see. Doesn't this make us look stupid?! Why are we watching celebrities act like idiots for entertainment? How are people who have done nothing of real value in their lives and only act like idiots suddenly becoming celebrities? It is like the travelling freak shows of the 19th century but we have the freaks piped into our house continually so that it almost seems normal. This is entertainment at a VERY high cost.

What about children who see this stuff all the time? Parents often use TV as a babysitter and are they monitoring what the kids are watching? Don't be naïve enough to think they don't change the channel when you leave the room. It will wear you out trying to keep an eye on how many times they flip the channel back and forth. If families do not spend enough time together doing real things, real activities and real conversations, this ridiculous garbage will become their reality. Send them out to play but don't let them get out of sight. The days are gone when parents can allow their kids to run the streets alone.

The typical commercial radio broadcast is atrocious. We can't put FM radio on in our car because the DJ banter is totally inappropriate for anyone under 16, if even then. What are we supposed to do about condom commercials at 3:00 in the afternoon? Are we supposed to explain this to a 7 year old? Thank god for MP3 players that plug into the car stereo. You can program hours of music that you are comfortable with and not worry. Satellite radio is a good option if you can afford the high subscription fees. You may have guessed by the subject of this book… I listen mostly to talk radio these days, 95% of the time the kids can listen to that. They may even learn something.

If the radio advertisers make no money from us, then, maybe that will begin to change things. The biggest problem here is that the group that is the most coveted by broadcasters, the 18-24 age group, generally has no children. Remember those days? They are still at an experimental age wanting to try many things their families might not approve of. They generally will not put a second's thought into the fact that children might listen to that broadcast and if they do will not be bothered by it because it is not their problem. These are the people the radio stations want to listen, and these products used by this age group are the ones advertisers want to put on these radio stations. It is a lose/lose for us parents. Luckily, as we said above, there are other options.

The FCC only acts when complaints are received so that is the only way to keep broadcast channels clean. If you see or hear something that really bothers you, give them a call. For cable channels we can use the V-chips in the television to block objectionable programs. Unfortunately there are only about 5 categories you can block so many borderline shows that are really OK for most children are blocked as well. History shows and animal shows are blocked due to violence or graphic images when we may not really have any issue letting a 10 year old watch these actual reality shows. So, except for small children who are to be limited to children's programming only, that is not a very effective option.

This is increasingly unpopular but increasingly important: There needs to be a family member present to take care of children, someone who is uncompromising in their desire to protect the children from harm and improper influences. Why do parents keep relinquishing control over their children to others in the most important times of their lives? Putting them in day care at 6 weeks old, who are these kids going to be bonded to, no one? They see day care workers 8-12 hours per day and their parents 2-6 hours. Who is teaching these kids their values? It is not the parents.

Letting kids age 13-17 stay home alone after school is probably more dangerous and damaging than the bizarre practice of putting infants in day care. Teenagers are mobile, crave freedom and are happy to try something new. As they get older they may like to shock their parents or prove to the crowd they are cool. With cramped neighborhoods and subdivisions with houses jammed on top of each other there are plenty of people to meet, many of whom you would never approve of. Worse yet many parents approve of their kids hanging with a pretty bad crowd. We've fallen that far.

Since most people today have no interest in getting to know their neighbors and having normal adult relationships with neighbors, parents have no idea who lives down the street from them. How many felons or juvenile delinquents live on your street? What about registered sex offenders? Don't you know?! Don't think there aren't any, you may find out the hard way. Go to www.familywatchdog.us put in your address and see what pops up.

Take a walk a few times a week and say hello. Get to know who is in what house and which houses no one ever comes out of. These you might need to ask about. Unfortunately your neighbors are pretty clueless too and you can't count on them to be honest. Some of these parents are those that you wouldn't approve of and they aren't going to admit that unless they don't realize how screwed up they are, but then at least, you'll know.

There are much worse influences on our kids which we won't get into. If we teach them well, keep them within arms reach, figuratively speaking, they should be OK. We're practicing "trickle up" morality. If we can affect all of the above then the more serious offenders will begin to lose their markets. Maybe we will again have enough people to stomp our feet and drive them out.

CHAPTER **10**

Fix Corrupt Governmental Practices

THERE ARE MANY ways that the federal government has been corrupt in their practices. Much of what they do is self-serving and often legislation is proposed that affects personal finances of the legislators. They set their own pay and benefits. Ethics violators recently have been given a censure and send back to their desks to legislate. Shouldn't they be looking for a new job?

Many leaders in organizations of all types practice "Scratch my back, I'll scratch yours" policies. That is normal, partners doing each other favors. The problem is when these practices affect impartiality and actually influence a person to neglect their responsibilities or knowingly make bad decisions. Campaign contributions have been a major influencer on this and fund raising takes up a huge amount of legislators' time.

This is a frequent complaint about Congress and even though seems to be corrupt there are reasons very little is done about it. For one, the Constitution states that a member of Congress cannot be arrested and prosecuted while in session. Looking at it today that may seem a stupid protection that they voted in for themselves, but not true. This was and remains a protection for members of Congress so that no government takeover can tear apart the house. In 1776 this was a huge worry for the founders of our government rebelling against England who were in fear for their lives for the treason against the king. This remains a valid reason to keep this provision alive and well, so we need to keep an eye on Congressmen and what they do, so that we can punish them with our votes. One way that the government has grown out of control is that congress uses loopholes in the constitution to pass laws they have no business being a part of.

Why don't we start a list? Here are a few to start you off....

Federal Stimulus packages

It has been said that much of the stimulus packages in 2009-2010 were for political paybacks for supporters during the 2008 elections. Case in point... Does it make sense that the great perpetrators of the financial collapse, supposedly big business and the banks were slammed for being at fault but were paid large amounts of stimulus money after the elections of 2008? Why?

Looking toward the elections of 2012 candidates will need to look at the debt situation in this nation and the basic struggles of the average American. There are currently over 400,000 Americans in debt collection. We are all well aware of the problems in the housing market and all the foreclosures going on around the nation. How could the government give a trillion dollars to banks and big business and ignore this? So much hand wringing is going on over how to fix the economy and stabilize the markets while so many tax paying Americans struggle with basic needs of food shelter transportation and security. Why is this being ignored when it is very much part of the answer to the problem?

I'm not saying that bailouts are a good idea, especially when the government is broke but since the money was spent; let's look at how it **should** have been used.

President Reagan talked about "trickle-down" economics. That is if you cut taxes to companies and employers then jobs and investment will progressively move on down to the workers. This is basic economics and makes sense. Sometime over the years too much faith was put in the big companies and executives who can take their money and run, leap with their golden parachutes and ride off into the sun. This is a major contributor to the economic crisis that we have been facing for the past decade. Keeping health insurance in the hands of the employers is a great competitive advantage for good companies and is a cost center that forces revenue into the hands of the employees. If the government has an issue with corporations taking too many profits, let them keep health insurance.

Many companies have eliminated stock options as compensation to prevent executives focusing on short term stock gain to boost their options at the expense of the long term solvency of the company. For instance, the CEO could buy or sell a division to boost the stock price for a few years but after the company loses the revenue that sold division would have produced or absorbs the financial struggles of their new acquisition; the executive has cashed in his options and left. The employees that remain are left to carry that burden minus a profit center or gaining an anchor.

How about trickle up economics? Rather than give the stimulus money to the banks, companies and state governments while we sit and wait for years for "shovel ready" projects that were not ready, to get underway. While the same banks who received this money work to get caught up with their foreclosure backlog, what about a one-time payment to the average American so they can get their own financial house in order? Think about it. One trillion dollars spent on stimulus and bailouts. Many are "shovel-ready" projects that took forever to actually begin if they have at all. Much of the money has not yet even been spent but we are paying interest on it every day. What happens when the projects are done? Are the jobs still there? If the jobs are gone at the end of the project and the foreclosures continue anyway, what's the point?

So, let's try this. Each tax-paying non-felon over the age of 18 gets a payment of $10,000 from the stimulus. What happens then? The government has invested a lot of time and effort in special programs for homeowners who are 90-days behind in their mortgages. Why wait for the foreclosures to come through while we spend more money. How many people have lost their cars and other collateral due to late payments? Credit card debt was at record highs at the peak of the crisis.

A $10,000 payment would allow everyone in trouble to get caught up. It would easily cover 90-days of mortgage payments and pay off probably half of all car loans. For those who have no car, it would cover the cost of a decent used car or a big down payment on a new one. Wiping out that much credit card debt will substantially reduce the monthly payment and interest accrual. Whatever a person's most painful financial issue, it could be solved or reduced significantly, life returned to normal and normal spending resumed rewarding well run businesses. This would stimulate the economy automatically.

For those who didn't have significant debt, they would instantly stimulate the economy by either investing the money or spending it. Restaurants, sports teams, travel agents, airlines, toy stores will all greatly appreciate the extra business and income for their employees.

Why did I qualify the eligibility for payment as tax-paying, non-felons over 18? Most people under 18 are high school students and are not filing their own tax returns or supporting themselves. In some cases there are independent 16 and 17 years olds and if they file their own tax returns as head of household or single and independent then they should also be eligible. Anyone who is responsible and has filed tax returns the past 2 years are eligible. Those who have not filed their returns: tough luck… no pay, no play. Those without proper respect for the process of collecting and paying taxes should not be eligible for a rebate. Felons are not eligible because committing a felony is a voluntary revocation of your rights to certain privileges in America such as: running for public office, becoming a lawyer or doctor and owning a gun. As the writer of this stimulus bill, I think it is only fair that the law abiding citizens get their reward, the felons are out. They are on their own. We need to provide more incentive to obey the law.

IPAB

Included in the outrage of the Obamacare bill railroaded through Congress with hardly a day's debate, here is another one for you.

In 2010, the Patient Protection and Affordable Care Act (PPACA) created the Independent Payment Advisory Board, or IPAB. When these unelected government officials submit a legislative proposal to Congress, it **automatically** becomes law!

PPACA **requires** the Secretary of Health and Human Services to implement it. How is that for taxation without representation?! What if that provision stinks and most of the American public is adamantly opposed? We don't get a say in it.

The Constitution requires the House, Senate and President to all review and concur on a bill before it becomes law. Now, we have un-elected bureaucrats making laws that bypass all review? How could anything be more corrupt?

CHAPTER 11

Attitude Adjustment-
Our future is up to you

WE ARE DUE for an old fashioned, proverbial Attitude Adjustment.

For starters, if we want this government and our country to get back on track we need to shift our thinking on how we view our government. We all know the famous quote by President John Kennedy about doing for your country instead of expecting the country to do things for you. People need to get back to taking care of themselves and others and not expect the government to take care of them.

If we want to shrink the "welfare state" and government spending then we need to take up the mantle and carry the load. Get involved in community organizations, charities, churches, Boy Scouts, Girls Scouts, schools. Start an organization of your own or take a turn at the food bank. Collect supplies or donate some extra cash. Take your kids with you teach them to get involved. Even if you only increase your involvement 1 hour per week, that is potentially well over 200 million extra hours of effort **every week** put toward helping others. Then, what would be left for the government to do?

Personally, I think if every child was involved in the Boy Scout or Girl Scout organizations in a well run Troop or Pack, most of this country's problems would disappear within a generation. If these children and their leaders all followed the Laws and Oath of these organizations throughout their lives we'd have nothing to worry about. Attending a religious service weekly to remind each of us how we are supposed to act wouldn't hurt either. No matter what the education, scouts, church or university, any learning needs to be put into practice to have any value.

Now, what is the American Dream that we all strive for? It is typically seen as the opportunity to work a full time job, have money to buy a house and a car and live in relative peace and harmony.

Some people have said The American Dream is dead and that life can't ever be like that again, like the 1950s and like the Cleaver family on TV. Very true, but life was never quite like the Cleaver's anyway. In the annals of history, how many of the years that Earth has been in existence have been like the 1950's?

Assuming the period of time we refer to ran 20 years from 1945 thru 1965 and that the period of recorded history is say, 6000 years, essentially, .333 % of human history actually resembled the 1950s. So, that lifestyle and supposed period of exceptional prosperity is an aberration, a blip on the radar screen and also a fond but faulty memory.

Nothing has changed in relation to the realism of the American Dream; it is the attitude and expectations of the American People that has changed. This is still a very achievable goal and is far from dead. The problem is that people born after the 1950s believe that this dream of lifelong achievement is now a **starting point**! They believe that people right out of college should have a fully furnished 2000+ square foot house, two new cars, a big screen TV, and day care for the kids, full health insurance and still free time to play on the weekends. Some people even think this is the starting point for a high school graduate and that the lament is that without high paying manufacturing jobs high school grads cannot have the jobs that enable the American Dream. This attitude needs to shift.

Look at workers from a third world country. As business opportunities expand and they see the opportunity to improve their lives, they are going to jump on it. They have no problem working long hours for short pay and probably in less than desirable conditions because it is an improvement for them. They have no issue with sacrificing to get an education because they never had anything to begin with. Few have the immense numbers of comforts and distractions that we have to take us away from work and education. We need to get used to being without these things and at least put them away for extended periods long enough to kick it up a notch and get it done when necessary. Do extra, trade some video game, TV and sports time for reading and study. Keep the hammer down because the traffic coming up in your rearview is getting very crowded.

A college graduate is entitled to nothing more than an entry level job in an industry that pays talented people better than others. This is assuming the student chose a major that relates to a good paying industry. Many students choose their major poorly and fair little better than a high school grad, though are going to be hired ahead of that person with only the high school education. There are exceptions in technical careers such as auto technician, electrician or nursing where the highly desired skills make a college education unnecessary to make a good living. College bound students need to recognize that the bachelor's degree is entry level. Higher education is needed to expect special advantages these days.

So, the realistic expectation coming out of college is actually to get a small apartment and a reasonably new used car. A married couple or family with 1, 2 or no children only needs a 1,000-1,200 square foot house with 2 or 3 bedrooms to start out.

I have seen people with only two children buying 3000 square foot, 5-bedroom house on a 1/8 acre lot and both parents working full time jobs to pay for it. Both parents have new cars and the kids are shuttled around pell mell from one activity to the next. All the while, the parents complain that the need two jobs just to get by, while with all these activities, it is really other people doing the parenting for them.

Realistically, this family could have a 1,200 square foot 2 or 3 bedroom house on an acre of land, one new car and one reasonable used one, maybe 3-7 years old. They could afford this easily on one income and have one parent stay home to actually parent. With an acre of land the kids could have plenty of activities and their parents would be there to participate at no additional cost.

When people try to keep up with the Smiths, (the Joneses are tired of people talking about them, they told me) everyone is trying to compete with a manufactured fallacy. Those who have not saved up or earned the income level to buy a home still want one. The politicians want their votes, so they create programs to get them one.

The Federal government mostly stuck to its constitutional boundaries until the 1920s or into the Great Depression where they began meddling with the economy, business and personal lives to the extent where the free market no longer exists. The normal checks and balances that keep an economy healthy are propped up with artificial band aids. When the economy says: "Bad news! People need to adjust their activities and spending habits; this trend has run its course.". The federal government says: "OH geez! People might be unhappy and not vote for us! Let's find a way to keep them appeased so they don't need to make any uncomfortable changes in their lives.". Well folks the time for uncomfortable changes have passed.

A perfect example is the housing market. People with low paying jobs could not afford houses and many complained that they were being discriminated against for various reasons including race, so back in the Carter Administration, in 1977, the federal government set up **Community Reinvestment Act,** a program where banks were not allowed to restrict credit to wealthier neighborhoods and had to offer credit to poorer neighborhoods as well. People with low end jobs could get houses more easily. Then, low money down, low interest rate loan programs were created. When banks were losing money on loans that were not profitable, Fannie May and Freddie Mac took them over and could deal in mortgage backed securities now known as "toxic assets".

President Clinton said he felt your pain so in 1995 he added to the housing mess by extending the Community Reinvestment Act to allow low-income people to qualify for homes they could not previously own. Then, with the 1999 repeal of the Glass-Steagall Act- the

Banking Act of 1933, banks were again allowed to deal in securities for the first time since the Great Depression. Now these "whole banks" as they are called, were partnered with Wall Street for the first time since 1933, allowing mega banks to exist again. By 2007, Fannie and Freddie owned or guaranteed nearly half of the $12 trillion U.S. mortgage market.

Now how much pain are we feeling? It is a shame while Presidents Reagan, Bush and Bush II were so focused on letting the markets work for themselves they did not correct the governmental mess that allowed it to occur. It has been reported though, that George W Bush tried 17 times to get Congress to reign in Freddie and Fannie but was shot down every time. John McCain also proposed a bill in 2005 to create more supervision for these entities but it was also shot down in Congress. If only Congress had cared more about the country and less about reelection, we would have a much better economy today.

When people without education need jobs, the federal government makes programs to entice construction and building so those people can work, so materials can be bought and sold, and so real estate can move.

What this does is creates an artificial market of buyers who cannot afford houses, who did not earn the income level necessary or save the down payment money. One of the crowning achievements of the American Dream is made available to people who haven't earned the right and attained that level of success.

Normally, a market corrects itself when houses reach a level that people are not willing to pay or cannot afford and buyers dry up. Housing prices drop and construction ceases until the value of the homes falls back into reality and people have the cash to buy.

In the artificial market interest rates are dropped and down payments waived until buying resumes. Once you have a situation where interest rates are near zero and houses are being sold no money down where do you go when that market saturates? The only option then is to start reducing home values until people can afford them again. People who bought houses at the top now are holding depreciated homes which in many cases they should never have been allowed to buy in the first place. If many of these people have lost their jobs or a portion of their incomes, they can't pay for the homes and foreclosures begin in mass numbers. Does this sound familiar?

Where does this stop? It stops when all of the people who can't afford homes have lost theirs or choose to sell them at a loss and buyers begin to buy again. This may leave many homes unsold for a long time or possibly demolished because there are more homes than buyers and the property is not being maintained and becomes unsalable. Once the number of homes falls to below the numbers of buyers, the prices will rise again.

The question is, will the government make the same stupid mistake again and allow unqualified people to buy homes again? Fannie Mae and Freddy Mac should begin reselling mortgages back to the private market and fold their doors. The banks will require down payments and good credit, rest assured. Interest rates could be manipulated by the government to spur buying but that would only be on sales to qualified buyers then. The government should get out of the business except to prosecute people guilty of fraud or discriminatory housing practices.

Moving forward by looking back.....

Almost a century ago in 1916, one of the first well known self help gurus in America, Reverend William John Henry Boetcker wrote a pamphlet known as "The Ten Cannots". In 1942 a pamphlet including his list and some quotes from Abraham Lincoln was printed up with Boetcker's name omitted. Since then, the list has been attributed incorrectly to Abraham Lincoln and was presented as such by President Ronald Reagan in at the Republican National Convention in 1992. This error does not change the sheer truth in what Reverend Boetcker said:

- You cannot bring about prosperity by discouraging thrift.
- You cannot strengthen the weak by weakening the strong.

- You cannot help little men by tearing down big men.
- You cannot lift the wage earner by pulling down the wage payer.
- You cannot help the poor by destroying the rich.
- You cannot establish sound security on borrowed money.
- You cannot further the brotherhood of man by inciting class hatred.
- You cannot keep out of trouble by spending more than you earn.
- You cannot build character and courage by destroying men's initiative and independence.
- And you cannot help men permanently by doing for them what they can and should do for themselves.

Boetcker also wrote the "Seven National Crimes"

- I don't think.
- I don't know.
- I don't care.
- I am too busy.
- I leave well enough alone.
- I have no time to read and find out.
- I am not interested.

One quote in that same 1942 publication that was actually from Lincoln has a similar theme: "Let not him who is houseless pull down the house of another; but let him labor diligently and build one for himself, thus by example assuring that his own shall be safe from violence when built."

So what to do....

Remember in any market you generally get paid what you are worth. Not what you feel you are worth but what you are worth to the market. It is what are you worth to others, your company, your country, what can you produce. The company has to remember this too because if you make yourself valuable, they need to recognize that, or someone else will.

How can people pull themselves up and build something for themselves? They really have no choice if the country is being run properly. For most of the past century and a quarter, labor unions and big manufacturing has created jobs that are long standing and secure. 30 year pensions were the norm. Outside of the Great Depression years in the 1930s, layoffs hardly occured anywhere for nearly 40 years. Those days are gone. The only thing building secure jobs is Big Government. They are not living in the same world as the rest of us and need to wake up.

General Douglas MacArthur said in the middle of this great time of security:" There is no security in this world. There is only opportunity."

Another quote from Abraham Lincoln: "The only security in this world is doing your job uncommonly well."

Those two quotes sum it up best. It is up to each person to seize on their opportunities and to be the best at what they do and to be more in demand than the people around them. This requires education and hard work, to avoid Boetckers Seven National Crimes and to be aware of what is going on around them. They must prepare for the future continually.

A recent study by the Brookings Institute released August 2012 shows that for jobs posted from 2006 thru 2012, there are more jobs than qualified candidates. Of current job openings in 100 major metropolitan areas, 43% require a minimum of a bachelor's degree. Only 32% of adults over the age of 25 actually have the credentials. Unemployment is greatest in the lower educated population. The jobs are there if you have the skills and credentials.

I've heard many people say that they cannot afford a college education or they don't have the time. There are all levels of truth to that because of different backgrounds, different family sizes and structures. Parents certainly have far less time than single people. Generally, step one of the process is to get your education first before you start messing around with starting a family or even participating in activities normally associated with starting a family. You set yourself up for a whole world of trouble and years of complaining if you screw up before you get out of the gate.

However, now, this next point flies in the face of what much of this book is about but as long as our Big Government is still in charge, most everyone can go to college nearly for free. Single people who say they can't afford it are simply ignorant of the process...or lazy. They also may need to borrow a lot of their money but once you have that good job you can pay it back at very low interest, so not a big deal. Pick a few schools, go to www.FAFSA.gov and get started with your financial aid application. A better future is only a few years away, and for those who have studied hard all their lives, private scholarships can take care of much of what you would normally need to borrow.

Be sure to study the world around you and to pick a major that people are willing to pay you for. Don't study Liberal Arts or Art History and expect to own a new luxury sports car some day. You'll need to shop the 100,000 mile and up lots, I'm sorry to tell you.

From there, you need to continually watch the economy. You won't get a big pay raise in a declining industry, you need to switch to a growing industry before you lose your job altogether. If you have a skill that is being replaced by robots, or computers you should probably study Robotics or Computer Science. Math or Science of any type is a great place to start. Most all high paying jobs value those skills. Then, while watching the markets during 4 or more years of college to see which industries have the best 20 year outlook, you can decide on a graduate degree that will put you in the driver's seat. Keep watching, keep changing, always be the first one with the hottest skill and you will never need to worry about your security again.

Everyone knows that computers and automation are taking over many industries but yet, college admissions to technology, science and computer programs have dropped almost 40% over the past decade. Are these kids paying any attention to the world around them? Furthermore, people start complaining about workers being brought from overseas on the H1-B Visas to do the work. If Americans don't want the jobs, workers need to come from somewhere. In the computer industry, consulting is a huge business. Many companies only need a specific skill for a short time maybe only once, or just for a few weeks. A wise company will not hire a new employee for this job but a good outsourcing relationship with consulting firm can provide lots of jobs for those who don't mind the variety of switching positions frequently while still having a steady paycheck.

Something struck me as a great illustrator of our problem... I read articles and watch news programs talking about thousands of people who have lost their jobs in numerous industries from all levels of the organization and all industries and one big thing strikes my mind....

If you have all of these unemployed people: salesmen, custodians, managers, accountants, engineers, programmers, manufacturing workers, Vice Presidents, CEOs, teachers, and on and on.... You have basically just listed the entire employee hierarchy of a large company. Why don't these people all sit down together and brainstorm a product or service they can make and sell! Then while they are all on unemployment compensation and have nothing to lose, start putting in 50 hour weeks to build this company. When the money starts coming in, just stop filing for unemployment and magically several hundred people are back to work, all on their own in an enterprise of their own creation. The government didn't need to do a thing.

Unfortunately, many groups of people just like this sit and complain that they can't find work, the economy is terrible, the government screwed everything up, and Wall Street screwed everything up. Are they taking classes on the government's dime during this time? Are they reading and studying the best skills to have. Why not get together with a bunch of other unemployed and BUILD something. At the worst you can add that to your resume and if the venture doesn't work out you can show up at your next job interview and explain your great idea and how your gumption provided you with new skills and experience.

If you do have a job, stop worrying about your future and blowing off steam playing video games. Your future is up to you.

As a matter of perspective, people in third world countries have very low rates of depression. Why is that? They are poverty stricken, wouldn't that make one miserable? Why are African and South American tribes dancing and singing and have celebrations? It comes down to expectations. All they expect out of life is food, shelter and togetherness and it takes up all of their time to achieve these few things. They are busy and satisfied.

Have you ever heard the phrase: "America runs on Xanax"? We get food and shelter on a silver platter and many people resent the presence of others encroaching on their space. So we have time to pursue other interests and worry about what other people are doing and getting. We pursue comfort and luxury, security, the latest gadgets, vacations and early retirement and if we don't have it all we get frustrated upset and depressed. The worst of us turn to corruption and crime to get what we didn't earn. The lazy ask the government to take care of them.

Maybe we need to look at our expectations. What did your grandparents have, and were they happy? Balance your expectations with your work ethic and see if you don't already have what you earned. Be satisfied with what you have and thrilled with the extras.

Conclusion

THOUGH THIS HAS been a long time coming and building slowly, with the elections of 2006 and 2008, I believe the country has begun its mad dash to the tipping point which will send it over the edge of the cliff. Elections of 2010 have begun to take the country back. What do we do in 2012 and beyond?

In summary:

1. Spending needs to be cut to below the tax revenue until the debt is gone.
2. Streamline Immigration so we can get quality workers in and eliminate the expense of illegal immigration and its drain on our national budget and its negative effect on crime rates.
3. Reform welfare, except in extreme cases of need people need to get back to work and not live for free on the back of the tax payers. Fraud needs to be eliminated
4. Make fair and simple tax code that does not penalize earning and investing but allows people to have more choice in how much tax they pay, based on the amount they choose to consume. Support families and quit penalizing our employers.
5. Health care costs need to drop through tort reform and increased competition in the markets. Single payer government run health care is a bad idea.
6. We do need to continue to work toward cleaner renewable energy but in the meantime use the existing energy more

effectively. Drill for new sources of domestic oil and take advantage of the abundant and CHEAP Natural gas.

7. Return business to businesses. Have smart regulation on the business community but let the free enterprise system do its job. Smarter taxation, less regulation and reform the Administrative structure to be fair to all.

8. United States Sovereignty. Protect our borders and our ability to regulate our people and laws within our borders without the Global movement dictating how we do it. Is there any country that is more capable of doing it right?

9. Fixing corrupt governmental operations includes all of the above. The government and the leaders of our country need to put the country and our people first. They are getting a salary and a pension. They need to earn it or get out.

10. Reversing Moral Decay is on all of us. We let this happen and we enable it. We need to start putting our foot down and stop it. Quit looking the other way or using it for easy entertainment. It is far too important.

11. Attitude Adjustment- Our future is up to you economically, socially and personally. Americans need to quit enjoying our comforts without taking into account where they came from and how fast they can go away. Keep the hammer down.

Nero fiddled while Rome burned. Will Americans continue to do the same? Do we wish to have the same fate as the Roman Empire? The financial woes of Europe are not far different from those of the United States. With our freedom of press and speech, Americans are supposed to be smarter than that. We should be aware of our surroundings and up to speed on the state of our government. The news media has failed us and the government is failing us. We should be angry at what is happening and too mad to take it anymore.

Alas, for the most, part we are not and when we are it is fleeting. We need to make changes to the way our government operates and how we as people see ourselves and act toward each other. We should hold our elected officials accountable for what they have done and keep the pressure on until it is fixed. In our culture of reality TV (which it actually is not), social media, internet escapism, network video gaming, headphone radios, I don't see it happening without a major change in personal attitudes. If we do not, we should be ashamed of ourselves and happily accept whatever fate we befall.

So let this book be the start of a discussion. Let's discuss the best ways to go about this repair of the United States. Propose new ideas or build on what we have here. If you have any evidence to add or to refute any of these ideas, I'm all ears. Don't forget to vote and hound your elected officials until they get it right or we are just blowing smoke without any fire.

So, Lets' get started......

Jeffrey P Gorman

Acknowledgements

THIS IS NOT a formal bibliography since the ideas presented in this book are a compilation of many years of news, radio and personal research. I cannot remember specifically where all of the ideas, facts and figures came from. I have noted my sources in the text where they are known.

Having said that I need to thank these people and organizations for their efforts and help along the way:

Staff and management of WBVP, WWKS radio in Beaver Falls, PA back in the day, especially John Nuzzo, Carl Anderson, Rita Maloney, Dimitri Vasillaros, Kyle Anthony and Bill Cameron for their tutelage and advice.

The on air personalities of KDKA radio in Pittsburgh, some of whom are also mentioned above. Also those at WBT radio in Charlotte with their fantastic list of talk hosts I've listened to over the past decade: Jason Lewis, Jeff Katz, Tara Servatius, Vince Coakley and John Hancock.

Of course the Faculty and Alumni of Clarion University, without whom, my involvement in the above may not have occurred.

All in all, too many people to name.

Also information gleaned from TV and print, CNN, Fox news, CNBC, Newsweek, Readers Digest. Discoverynews.com, National Geographic

And research done by the Bureau of Labor Statistics, Environmental Protection agency, Department of Health and Human Services,

Center for Immigration Studies, Cato Institute, Brookings Institute, Federation for American Immigration Reform, Heritage foundation, American Gas Association, Colorado School of Mines, Massachusetts Institute of Technology

My MBA Professors at Wingate University: Attorney Robert N Burris whose Business Law class at Wingate University caused this book to take a minor left turn at Albuquerque and some major scope creep from some great perspective on the Constitution and the men who wrote it. Dr. George Stratis whose Business 500 "Firehose Economics" course gave me the kick in the pants to start actually start writing the book.

Special thanks to the folks at Family Dollar Stores, my home for the past 10 years and all of those who have supported my family in these last difficult months.